Trail Mix

Hold the Chemo

Trail Mix
Hold the Chemo

By Jeffrey Norman Ide

ISBN 978-0-557-49726-3

For my Mom whose dream was to one day write a book. This one's for you, Barb.

_ Jeff

Introduction

This book is a compilation of blog entries from my late husband Jeff during his fight with brain cancer. They are random thoughts, memories and stories from Jeff's life and how he approached everything with humor and a strong sense of faith. He holds nothing back as he shares his daily experiences and struggles. You will find his humorous insights, throughout his journey with this relentless disease, an inspiration. Jeff never wanted to come across as preaching so his vision and goal was to reach people and draw them nearer to God. He always said, "Laughter is good medicine but add God to the mix and the heart smiles!"

Jeff and I were always committed to God's plan no matter the outcome. I am confident that God's plan is perfect and I hope to see it unfold some day. The hardest part has been going forward without him. I really miss our coffee breaks. I miss his voice and how he said my name, his laugh, his dance moves, his smell. I miss his sense of humor and how he made us laugh. I just plain miss everything about him. I really didn't realize how much he kept us entertained until he was gone. He was right, laughter heals your troubles so I try to find humor in **almost** everything. I often think of his favorite verse, especially the part about being thankful in **ALL** circumstances. It seems impossible, but I've learned feeling thankful and being thankful are two different things. Just be thankful and the feeling will soon follow. We are better people and closer to God today because of Jeff and we feel so grateful and honored to have been chosen to be part of his story.

- Diane Ide

It was August of 2007 and I had just moved back to Michigan from Florida. The next day my father went to the hospital, and we found out that he had a tumor in his brain. At the time we really didn't know the severity, but since then my life was changed. For the next 22 months I saw him go through the hardest thing anyone could imagine. Through two surgeries, six weeks of radiation, the continuous treatments and him not being able to do the things he loved was the hardest. There were good days and bad days, and I am glad for the time that we had together before that day in June.

During this time I was working a really early morning shift at work, so I would be up and ready for work at 3 a.m. He would be up blogging and we would have coffee before I left. I could tell he just wasn't the same person, but he had a thankful heart and made the best of everyday. This was extremely difficult for me, and I know it was for him too. We all knew the day would come, but it was far too soon. My father was the greatest person I ever knew, and I am thankful that he was my father. He taught us all very valuable life lessons, and his stories are by far some of the best I have ever heard. He was a great person and will be missed by everyone who ever knew him.

- Andrew Ide

Living with my father during the time of his sickness was tough. I think it is tough for anyone who has a loved one with cancer. Life was a lot different during the years of his sickness. It was as if I was living with someone I didn't know. It was hard to watch as the tumor grew. Slowly it took a little bit more of my dad. I believe it affected everyone he came in contact with. Amazingly, his love and sense of humor were unaffected. He made people appreciate their lives better. He also brought people closer together, and from all over America too, through love, friendship, and blogs. He will be loved and missed by all.

- Brett Ide

Chapter One

On August 27, 2007 I heard these words. " Jeff, we don't have good news for you." The Doctor continued, "The CT scan shows a tumor as you can see here." I glanced over at the scan he was holding and could clearly see, even with my lack of medical knowledge, that there was a golf-ball sized object in my head. I quickly concluded that it probably didn't belong there. The doctor said, "We'll send you down for an emergency MRI," a procedure and word that has become part of my everyday vocabulary. The MRI confirmed what the CT scan had shown. I knew the MRI team could see the monitor during the scan because, after the MRI was finished, I could see in their faces that they saw something. They were probably wondering what a Titelist 3 was doing in my head?

OK, the first thing I needed to do was call my wife, Diane. I had just dropped her off at the airport a few days earlier so she could go to Tennessee and help her Grandfather, who was ill. Immediately after receiving the bad news I called her from the emergency room. When she answered the phone, the combination of the tears and the word "tumor" would not allow me to produce any sound that she could understand. Finally, I was able to let her know that I had some bad news. She immediately began setting up a flight back to Detroit, which I took great comfort in.

At 43 years old, and very active, I didn't really understand how this would affect my family and me. It was just last week that I was riding my Harley through the Straights of Mackinaw to Sault Saint Marie, Michigan in a driving rainstorm. In a few weeks I would be off to California and Norway for business. So, what could stop me?

I should bump back a few months to the spring of 2007 when Diane and I were having some difficult times due to the affects of this tumor that was growing in my brain. Of course, at the time, I had no idea it was there. As it grew, it was gradually pushing on the grey-matter and causing slow and subtle changes in my behavior. Diane mentioned, on more than one occasion, that I was acting like an "air-head" and that I needed to see someone to get some mental help. Each time I could laugh it off because I thought I was "normal." By the time I reached the ER in August, I had a shopping list of behavioral changes that I had noticed, such as mild vision changes, mild hearing changes, fatigue, loss of appetite, sudden urges to cry, confusion, difficulty driving, a confrontational attitude, not enjoying talking with people, and a general dislike of life. Once I listed these out, I knew in my heart of hearts that I was in trouble. While I was sitting in the ER, a Tim McGraw tune came to mind and it goes something like this...

I was in my early forties with a lot of life before me, then the moment came and it stopped me on a dime. And, it mentions that there is a lot more living to do. But, with what little I knew of cancer, I figured I could probably be dead in days. Cancer in the brain doesn't sound all that good. Will it explode before I get to surgery? Oh man, this is definitely something I didn't sign up for. Why me? My Mom, during her battle with M.S., would always say about herself, "Why NOT me." But all I could think is why me? After giving

Diane the life-altering news, I called my youngest sister Stacey to let her know what's going on and where I was. I just needed another set of ears to share this with, and she came to mind.

The ER nurses loaded me up with steroids to reduce the swelling and then released me into the hands of two beautiful angels, our eldest son Andrew and our youngest son Brett. At the time they were 22 and 17 respectively. I was so glad to see them that day. I know they we're more confused than I was, but I had no clue as to what I could expect or, what they could expect. But, I would soon learn.

One thing I did learn is that everything in my life that I thought was important suddenly became unimportant. And, the things I thought were unimportant became the center of my life. My relationships with Jesus Christ and family and friends became paramount. I was seeing the world through new eyes and I was afraid of getting healed and leaving this new place. I was thanking the Lord for everything. I think I found what having a relationship with Christ is all about.

The first medical opinion that Diane and I received was that it was probably cancerous and they could treat it with a chemo-disk after the majority of the tumor was removed. They mentioned a life expectancy of a few months to a few years! We were encouraged to get a second opinion, so we did and we received pretty much the same news. And, we were given some options on some clinical trial drugs that were not FDA approved yet.

My first surgery was performed on September 15, 2007 and everything went as well as could be expected that day. From the time I checked in on that Thursday to the time I was discharged, 53 hours had passed. I say I set a world record but I really doubt that I did. All I knew was I wanted to get out of there and get home as soon as possible. My recovery at home was a good time to bond with Diane and the boys and to work on my relationship with Jesus Christ. My hour-long Bible time every morning was long over due. I haven't missed a day since my diagnoses. One of my fears was that I would start to feel "normal" and return to my previous self. I would rather have the tumor in my head than the old Jeff. What I'm saying is that the old Jeff's relationship with Christ was very distant and now that I was more focused on Him I didn't want to lose that. To be honest, the closeness I felt on day one and the closeness I feel today is different. It seems hard to stay so close to Christ because the pressure of the world is always pressing in on me. You know, bills, the kids, the unknown, etc... Hmm!

One week after my surgery, my Neurosurgeon Dr. Rock, called with the pathology report. It was exactly as he had expected. The diagnosis was Glioblastoma Multiforme 4, (GBM), which is the most malignant, aggressive and deadly form of high-grade astrocytoma. GBMs are the most common brain tumors in adults. They make up approximately half of all astrocytomas. They can occur at any age but are more common in older patients. Wow, this diagnosis didn't sound good, and it wasn't. Now what? My world is falling apart. I always figured I would be wiped out in a car or motorcycle accident. I never imagined it would be cancer, let alone brain cancer. From where I was standing it seemed like a suicide bomber had a higher probability of living than I did.

Wow, my future looked bleak. Bleak? Bleak would explain the difference between a ball game getting rained out and the whole stadium falling down. Either way the game is cancelled. But, in my case, the stadium was lying in a pile of rubble. Either the suicide bomber didn't like the long lines at the men's room or one of the teams that were playing that day. But, in either case, he decided to press the red button on his belt. The bottom line was pretty simple. Jeff has brain cancer so what is he going to do about it? Could he give it back? I know he didn't want it. I'm pretty sure I would have remembered him telling the host "yes, I'll take brain cancer for two hundred please." Name something that Jeff did not sign up for? Yes, I think I would have remembered this exchange. Thinking back I would have probably chosen the special belt with the red button. Anyway, this is what I'm left to deal with.

Before my first brain surgery I asked my wife Diane to be sure she gave me the news from the doctor as soon as I woke up. She and my older brother Victor were given that task. Since he is hearing impaired I'm not sure he was the best selection to relay the news from the doctors. Since Vic is a corporate Human Resources guy he was selected. Back in the day, when he wore clogs and a denim jump suit, we may have bypassed him and selected Ann-Marie, my other sister. Ann-Marie is 13 months older than I am so I'm guessing that Mom and Dad didn't read the take-home pamphlet after she was born. Ann-Marie is the accountant in the family and puts a lot of thought into everything. My younger sister Stacey would have been a good choice to deliver the news too since she is a teacher and very detail oriented. My folks had four children with only 5 years between the oldest and the youngest and we are all very close. We always played well together in the sand box. I was always the square-peg sibling that tried to fit into the round hole. We were all college educated but, what took them four years, took me 13. They followed the conventional college route and I crammed my four years of college into thirteen by working full-time, marrying Diane when I was twenty years old, and raising a family along the way. The good news is that Diane and I are still together nearly twenty-five years later. She has been my best friend and my rock and I could never thank her enough. So, when I received my engineering degree, I was pretty pleased. Not a whole lot smarter, but glad to have that part of my life behind me. If I had to do it again I wouldn't change a thing. Diane and I are blessed with two fine young men, Brett and Andrew. We feel truly blessed by God as we look back and reflect on life.

My siblings and I grew up in rural Michigan and there was always plenty to do around the farm. Usually I would end up finding some way to terrorize my sister Stacey like locking her in the milk-house when she was four years old and then forgetting she was in there. Or, the time I put a down-filled vest on her and took pot shots at her with my bb gun. I thought it was a good idea at the time but my Mom didn't! Maybe she beat this tumor into my head. I don't know. Mom was a wonderful lady and I'm sure any beating I got was necessary. Maybe a beating is the wrong word but a stern spanking just doesn't seem to do it justice. But, as a parent, I know it was what I needed.

My mom has since passed away from Multiple Sclerosis. She was diagnosed in 1981 and died in 2007. She taught me so much about life and I find myself drawing on her wisdom as I fight this battle with cancer. Dad was a motorcycle cop in his younger years and worked in the local schools as Mr. Fix It before he passed in 2003 from an Aortic Aneurysm. He was the "deal with it guy." I am able to combine both of their strengths and battle on. Since they both knew that laughter was a great coping mechanism, I can only find humor in everything I look at. This keeps me sane or, should I say, alive?

So, getting back to my surgery. I wanted to know if it was cancer and whether I would be all right. I know this is a slippery slope for family members but I really feel that they owe it to the patient if requested. Going through this process, I feel it is best for the family to report the facts and not sugarcoat it or beat around the bush. Cancer is not fun but knowing the facts is important. The family shouldn't be all gloom and doom but supportive and honest. Let the patient own the illness and you'll probably find out they're stronger than you think. Thinking back, I'm now concerned that Victor was part of the family medical update team. We all know Victor. When I think of the moment I saw him after surgery I'm surprised that he didn't say "hey Jeff, you'll be OK but you have a whole lot of blood in your head bandage. Wow, it's even way down on your neck and shoulders too. Dang bro, does it hurt?" He'd say, "It looks like you got in a gang-fight but forgot your gang. Wow, your head is all jacked-up!" Vic has always been a glorified storyteller but that's why we love him.

Anyway, as I was waking up in the Recovery Room I asked, "Ok, what is it?" The next thing I hear is the swoosh of the cloth room divider slide open and I hear a voice. "Hi Mr. Ide, I'm Brittney and I'll be your nurse. I'll continue to talk to you but I won't use my indoor voice. Let me turn this interrogation lamp on first so I can shine it in your eyes. Are you having any pain? One being none and ten being real bad! O.K., I'm going to yank your catheter out now so, when I say three, just cough. It looks like a small one so it shouldn't hurt at all. We had to special order one for you! OK, three!" "Ouch!" I yelled. I think I heard myself yelling, "Code blue, code blue! Ten, ten, ten!!" Anyway, if a patient can endure that aggressive wake up they can handle any audible news you throw at them. So, keep it real and deliver it with love. Be supportive through the process. If you don't know something, tell them that too.

Chapter Two

Thoughts

Posted Jan 28, 2009 4:16am

I'm thankful that you all found my first story somewhat humorous because I think we all need something to laugh about. It's a great outlet for me, as I know that things could always be worse. As I've said, "A little brain cancer never killed anybody…. but it will when you get a whole bunch." Sounds like a good title for a book??

My life has been one blessing after another and I have no regrets, except the time I locked my baby sister (Stacey) in the milk house when she was four years old. I was a couple years older than her. I still carry the physical and emotional scars from what happened after Mom found out. I can honestly say I have never, nor ever will, lock someone in a milk house again. Whew, I think Mom meant business!!

During this cancer treatment, I have had an outpouring of love and support from my family, friends, cousins, aunts, uncles, and work associates. And, the list goes on and on. Even the neighbor brought over a loaf of zucchini bread. My oldest son, Andrew, calls him (the neighbor) Sweeney Todd (from the Johnny Depp movie) because the guy is always cutting stuff up in his garage with a power saw at weird hours of the night. Andrew thinks he's dismembering people. Yikes! I told Andrew where the bread came from and then told him I thought I found a toenail in it. We had a few good gut laughs over that one. We're thankful for the bread and thankful for the laughter. Still, I was blessed by his thoughtfulness in bringing the bread. You've got to hand it to him. Get it? Hand it to him? Anyway, if any of you are in the neighborhood, please stop at our house for a piece of zucchini bread. I'll sort through it and make sure I get all of the toenails out of it.

I think I'll try and do something crazy during chemo tomorrow so I can leave the nurses with something to think about. I'm thinking something about the urine sample cup and some apple juice. I've been planning this for a while and tomorrow may be the day. I'll let you know. I love you all and may God continue to bless you all. – Jeff. Diane gets a break from me today because Stacey is taking me to treatment. I'll add some additional thoughts as the day and days progress. We have had some home break-ins in the area lately and I understand that they are stealing medicine. So, I think I will comment on this topic. J
Enjoy the day. God bless you all. – Love Jeff

Posted Feb 4, 2009 3:16pm

Hi All - I thought I was losing some more hair from the chemo but I found it. It was on my pillow. I saw the hair and thought we bought a cat. But, the hair was mine. I asked Diane if I could now wear my leather cowboy hat? She said

Nope! Hmm. Maybe I'll act a little goofy and wear it. I'll blame it on the tumor. I'll have to work on the acting goofy part since I'm so levelheaded. On second thought, my head is not really level. This might take some more thought on my part. News: Getting ready to go on a 3-day trip with Diane and my siblings to Nevada. The Hoover Dam is on my bucket list so I'll be able to check that one off. We'll get home on Sunday. I'm really looking forward to it. Maybe I can terrorize Stacey at the Grand Canyon? I can do my Frankenstein thing. We'll update with photos and some good stories when we return. God bless you all and have a great weekend. I love you all. - Jeff

Chapter Three

The Wedding

Posted Feb 9, 2009 3:21pm

We made it back from Las Vegas last night. We had a great time with Vic, Mike, Ann, Stacey, and Prashant. The Hoover Dam was an awesome site to see. Also, Mike, Stay, Vic & Ann arranged for Diane and I to renew our wedding vows for our 25th Anniversary. And yes, we did it at the Graceland Wedding Chapel!! (Mike & my sibs) They're all crazy! Oh, and Elvis performed the service. So, the boys can now say that their Mom & Dad ran off to Vegas and got married. We had such a nice time and I am truly blessed with great brothers & sisters!! Diane & I are really thankful that they could all make the trip. We'll upload some photos & stuff when we get them organized! Viva Las Vegas!!

Vic, Ann-Marie, Stacey & Mike, Diane & I are so blessed that you all made the trip to Vegas with us. We had a great time. Please know that we love each of you so very much and you are very important to us. Thanks for arranging the Wedding!! :)). We Love You All!! God has truly blessed us with each of you. Or as I say, All Y'All!! Love J & D!!

Getting' Hitched

Posted Feb 10, 2009 10:03am

Thanks for the kind words on our wedding vow renewal after 25 years. With all the steroids I'm on I look pregnant with my baby-bump. I think the Vegas chapel folks thought Diane knocked me up and we had to shotgun the wedding. The Vegas trip & Hoover Dam was on my "bucket list" so I can check that one off. Thanks again to my brothers & sisters! More photos to follow. Love Jeff.

Chapter Four

MRI - Update

Posted Feb 11, 2009 5:34pm

Today was my MRI day. The scan showed that the tumor is progressing (growing) but the growth is very small. The Tumor Board (you remember those guys at Henry Ford Hospital) would like me to continue with the Avastin but change to a new I.V. chemo and stop the Temodar chemo pills. The new stuff is called Carbo Platt. Sounds like a new workout video! Clinically I'm doing really well. My strength, blood work, blood pressure, lack of seizures, etc. is all good. So, I'm doing better than most. I thank the Lord for this. Amen! Steroid dosage will be reduced a little bit.

As soon as Diane & I got to treatment today the nurse had us sign some forms regarding some side effects from an earlier study I was on. Yeah, some guy had some side effects from being on it. "What kind of side effects," we asked? "He died," she said. So, I guess he's out of the study group? (Bless his heart). Hmm, kind of a heavy-duty side effect don't ya think? OK, I'll sign the form! I'm thinking with my new Carbo-Platt workout routine I'll avoid this side effect? Note to self - buy new leg warmers and a headband. Also, a T-shirt that says "Ditch the Phat, Do the Carbo-Platt." All in all, my scan was good. Ann-Marie thanks for meeting Di & me for lunch at the hospital. It was nice seeing you! God bless you all and thank you Lord. Next MRI will be in a couple months. I'm grateful for all the things I'm able to do! Still enjoying life, but this Brain Tumor is MAKING ME THIRSTY! Not really, but it was a funny line from Seinfeld. These peanuts are MAKING ME THIRSTY!

Chapter Five

Happy Valentine's Day

Posted Feb 14, 2009 9:03am

Hi All, just a quick note. Everything is going well. I feel like a million bucks! (All green and wrinkly) Not really, I'm doing great. I see the snow falling and wish I were back in Vegas. Although I'm reconsidering getting on another airplane! There was sad news out of Buffalo today where that plane crashed. We're very sad and our prayers go out to the crew and passengers!

For me, the prayers are working, so keep them coming. I am really grateful I can do the things I can do. There are so many folks that are limited by their illnesses but I am fortunate to be plugging along. So, I don't have one complaint. OK, one. I had to clean the kitchen today. Why does Diane work me so hard? :)). I tell her I'm not just another pretty face around here!! She tells me, "Don't blame the mirror for what it reflects." What is she trying to tell me?? Remember, I'm working with half my brain tied behind my back! :)) Thanks again for the kind words and prayers. God is good all the time! I'll talk at you all later. Love Jeff.

Chapter Six

The Hospital - A humorous look

Posted Feb 17, 2009 7:30pm

A word that has become commonplace around our home is Henry Ford. This is the hospital where I've been getting my treatment and where I had both of my brain surgeries. Our family refers to it as "Hank" because we seem to know Henry a little too well. It's quite a place. They have valet parking and everything.

The first observation I made today was on the elevator. Everyone was checking everyone else out to see what ailment they had. When the elevator doors open, there is a large sign on each floor that announces to the world why you're there. So, we're heading up and the door opens. The sign says BRAIN CANCER. You'll have to throw those people out because they'll just stand there all day saying huh, wha'? Then, the 12th floor doors open and the sign reads "COLON DAMAGE DUE TO NEGLECT" and the next group files out. We all sigh, thankful that's not our floor. Next stop - 9th floor, DISODERS OF THE SPINE. Again, these folks head out and we all know why they're at the Hank. Then, 3rd floor MENTAL DISORDERS. Hey, let the guy out who keeps screaming "Hooo Ya!" I knew he was a "Third Floorer". 2nd floor, HYPOCHONDRIACS. These folks may decide to jump out on any floor. If there is any shame in your disease, I recommend taking the stairs.

Anyway, the Hank is a huge campus and you will see all kinds of people there. Lots of lab coats too. The nurses and doctors are all real nice, but why wouldn't they be? "Hey, here comes Jeff"… Cha-ching. "Quick, get me a box of the twelve dollar band-aids. We'll give him two today!" I noticed that sometimes, after I've had surgery, I find rectangular shaped areas on my body that have an unusual black funk. I think to myself "Oh, it's an U.B.Z." - Unknown Band-Aid Zone, which means I didn't know one was there and some crazy body funk started to grow. It's not real pretty, but what's a boy to do? Once, after surgery, they told me that I had to be able to walk the halls before I could leave, so that's what I did. After this last brain-surgery, my eyesight was a little off. But, I walked anyway. I came to a door that had a sign that read "Live Plants Only" but I thought it said Live "Patients" Only. It was kind of creepy. It reminded me of my first brain surgery. They call the surgery a Craniotomy. When the nurse was flipping through the book, I thought the page said Crematorium. I said, "Whoa, go back a page. Did that say Crematorium?" After I quit laughing she looked at me like I was insane. Hmm, what floor was that?

Some of the specialty areas in the hospital are named after the family members of Henry Ford such as Josephine Ford Cancer Center, etc. I always wonder about the Ford lady they named the Sleep Disorders Clinic after. She must have been lazy or laid around all day. I bet they had a good laugh at her expense when they were assigning the disorders to the family?

Now, getting to the hospital is a job in itself. It's 65 miles one way from our home and there is no easy way to get there. Any treatment or visit is a daylong field trip. "Hey, can you come in on Monday and we'll change your band-aid? We notice this one is growing some fur." Oh man, another UBZ got past me. I should really switch to duct tape and a cotton ball. The cotton balls are only a dollar a piece or three-for-five dollars. Duct tape I have at home and can maybe smuggle a roll or two in! "Is that a roll of duct tape in your pocket or are you just happy to be here?" I knew I could work that lame phrase in somewhere!

Well, that's kind of a thumbnail of the Hank. Watch out for Live Patients and don't go near the Crematorium! God Bless You All and I'll be back in touch. Thanks for the prayers. I asked the doctor during my last visit if they put locks on the exam doors because people were dying to get in. Hmm, he didn't laugh. I'll drop that line on him the next time I see him to see if he lightens up. I told him that I must be looking bad because, when we drove by the cemetery, two guys with shovels started chasing me.

I thank my Lord for every new day and for the people in my life He has blessed me with. I'm a lucky boy and could not make it through this without Him.

Have a blessed day. I love You All - Jeff

Chapter Seven

Drivers Training, again

Posted Feb 19, 2009 4:33am

Yesterday I practiced my driving. Diane needed to do some grocery shopping, so I volunteered to help and offered to drive. I have been practicing by looking out of my right eye only in hopes of compensating for the loss of my peripheral vision. I guess that would explain why I have a whole lot of bruises on my left side. I seem to be running into the cupboard doors, chairs, doorframes and the usual household obstacles. I can tell when Diane is mad at me because she'll rearrange the furniture!! Anyway, we get in the car and I pray for a safe journey, but I still look over to make sure she has her seat belt on. Kind of like Pastor Mark would say, "If you're in a boat and a storm comes up, pray to God but start rowing for shore". Well, here we go. I navigate my way onto the freeway and safely avoid our mailbox, so things are looking good. It's a little stressful but we get to the store. This is a good sign but I know I need more practice.

I compare my driving to my friend Duane. I'll avoid throwing him under the bus here because he'll never stop by for coffee if I "out" him. When I ride with him, I usually put on a toe-tag so I can help the EMS guys sort out the wreckage a little easier. The first time I rode with him he had me lock the door. I thought he was concerned for my safety, but I soon realized he was concerned that I might jump from the moving vehicle. I understand that before most accidents a driver will call out the name of Jesus. In Duane's case he would say, "Hey, hold my Mountain dew, I'm gonna try something." Sorry Duane. Hey, why don't you stop in for a coffee, or did I blow it? I guess after my driver's training I'm not sure I'm ready for the road yet. I think I still need some practice but I won't give up. I told the doctor he needs to get me to spring time so I can ride my Harley. And, in order to ride my Harley, I need more practice driving. So, that's what I'll continue to do. I'll learn to drive with these eyes.

Yesterday I was surprised that no one reported a drunk-driver on the road. I had all the telltale signs. I maintained a slingshot speed between 55 and 65 mph. I would randomly tap the brakes for no explainable reason. I sat forward in the seat with both hands on the wheel in the 12 and 5 positions and, thanks to the steroids, I have a nice red glow on my face. Besides that, I would swerve within my lane without notice. Hmm, I may have to ask Diane to start locking her car door too. And, maybe putting a toe-tag on her would save time?

I'll keep praying for improved eyesight and maybe one day I'll have a lot more of my independence back. I'll let you know how it's going. Be blessed and have a great day. – Love Jeff. Oh, sorry Duane. Don't take offense to my ramblings. I'm sure it's the tumor talking. The "old" Jeff would never "out" you like that! Yea, this tumor is talking all-kinds of crazy. It has to be, because you know I would never say these things! Right??

Chapter Eight

Brain Tumor - What's it Like?

Posted Feb 19, 2009 6:15pm

"So, what's it like to have brain cancer" I've been asked. "Do you hear an echo inside your head when you talk? Does it itch? What's it all about?" Well, I tell everyone that it does itch and the only way to reach it is through my nose. I figure this is a good excuse to be able to pick my nose and get away with it. My only problem is that I'm not sure where to wipe it. The one I left on the edge of the grocery cart was not well received by the bag boy. The one under the chair in the doctor's office, I'm sure, will be received with just as much excitement when they find it. I guess I could just leave it on my finger but then I'd have to hold in a strange way. I think if they flicked off a little easier I could just fling it, but I think the chemo has some type of adhesive properties that would put super-glue to shame. It's really embarrassing when I flick it but it flings in a different direction. Who knows where that one will end up?

Do I hear echoes when I think? What, huh? Who said that? OK, I can honestly say that I don't hear any echoes, but the voices are getting louder. "Jeff, scratch your tumor, your tumor, tumor, tumor, tumor.. "Pick it and flick it." Hey, sounds like a new idea for a game show. Maybe, but they say try not to sit in the front row and never touch under your seat. Ok, so there doesn't seem to be any echoing going on. Well, none I care to admit. Can I use the tumor to my advantage? I need to be able to gain something by being the host to this crazy thing.

I sometimes wonder if I make people panic when I mistype a word in an email. Do they say, "Oh look, he ain't right. The tumor is eating him up from the inside and he's forgetting everything he has ever known." Or, do I spell that nown?? Who nose how to spell that one? When Diane asks me to do the dishes I will actually get in the sink and ask, "What's a dish look like?" This action will usually get me out of the task. Sometimes, if I just keep repeating the word "dishes" for a few minutes, this will also get me off the hook. I don't like doing the dishes because it interferes with my tumor scratching episodes. I only wish I had smaller fingers or a larger nasal cavity. It's a good thing I don't have colon cancer, although the lady with the three little kids at the mall was probably thinking I did. I tried to duck for cover but those darn teenagers at the sunglass kiosk were blocking my path. Every few steps I had to snap my knee to the side to make sure I kept a somewhat natural stride. I must have looked like Gabby Hayes from the old westerns!

Hang on. I think I hear someone. Oh wait, it's just me again but I forgot what I said to myself. It sounded like "find a snack in the cupboard". Hey, that sounds like a great idea but, once I figure out what a cupboard is, will I be able to identify one of these so-called snacks? The last snack I think I ate was wrapped in see-thru paper, was yellow, very greasy, and had a picture of a young Mexican lady on it. Boy, I won't eat that again. Andrew and Brett kept calling me butter-breath for the rest of the day.

Hang on, this tumor needs to be scratched again. I do not be knowing why it be itching so much and it is hard to type with three fingers. I remember after my diagnoses I called my brother Victor to tell him the news. He heard from Diane, or one of my sisters, that I had a brain tumor. But, he hadn't talked to me yet. I said, "Hellwo Bictor, Dis is Deff. How ur yo do in? I do in petty gooood." The phone was silent from his end. He must have thought my brain was being eaten up from the inside. I figure a little shock to his person would do him good. I mean, he was my older brother and paybacks are heck!

Maybe if I talk like this at the "Hank" I'll get a better spot on the elevator? I'm the idiot that gets in the elevator and politely moves to the side but every time I end up leaning against all the buttons. So, we end up making a courtesy stop on every floor. When all the passengers look at all the buttons I lit up, and then at me, I point to my head and say, "I'm going to the 13th floor." They realize I'm not playing with a full deck and settle in for the long ride. Maybe next time I'll just stand there rocking back and forth repeating to myself "Brain Tuma, Tuma, Tuma." Maybe they'll cut me a break? You know, I could even itch it for an added affect? I could even shout out " this tumor is making me thirsty!" I'll try 'em both and see what works best.

I'm going to sign out for now. I know that the Lord has blessed me with another day and I give Him thanks for that. He is truly in charge. Everyone, have a blessed day. Love Jeff. Thank you all for your prayers and kind words. I do read them all and truly value them. I sea u lator.

Chapter Nine

Trail Mix - No Thanks!!

Posted Feb 20, 2009 5:15am

Up and at it early again. It seems like I'm ready to get my day started at 4AM these days. I find this to be great prayer time and some good quiet time with God. Diane will get up in a few hours and get me started on my meds. I know its called medicine but I feel smarter when I use the doctor-lingo, Meds. I have noticed that my meds are starting to resemble paint-chips. Diane says she doesn't write the script, she only dispenses them. "Script". Hey cool word. Should I be looking closer at these paint chips she is giving me? I'm not sure. My Mom used to let me chew on my crib and I turned out all right. Maybe the whole lead paint thing is an old wives tale. In all seriousness, if the med distribution were left up to me I'd be in a world of hurt. Remember, I was the guy who ate the stick of butter and the trail mix... let me explain that one. I've been contemplating blogging on this next topic but maybe I can delicately communicate it.

During our trip to Vegas I kind of got my internal plumbing out of whack. My biggest mistake was eating the four pounds of trail mix on the airplane. I was very selfish with it. I pretty much ate the entire bag. OK, if you can imagine stuffing a pipe with trail mix and then pouring in a couple of bags of Chemotherapy juice, you can probably understand where I'm going. Yep, straight to the Emergency Room. Boy, sitting across the desk from the registration nurse explaining why I'm there was a pretty humbling experience. But, at this point, there was no shame in my game. I told her to hate the play not the player! She got me registered and sent me to an examination room.

The next thing I know Nurse Bob, with the fat fingers, comes into the room. Great, a new person I can tell my trail mix story to. I figured he probably heard about me when he was in the cafeteria. But, maybe he can humiliate me a little more since I can't walk by this time. I thought I could find a wheelchair and make my exit but I couldn't sit either. So, Bob tried to make me feel comfortable. He said the chemo would do that. OK Bob, I also ate four pounds of trail mix. You know the one's with the chocolate candy in it. So, I told Nurse Bob (yep, with the big fingers) that I think my butt is broken. "Yea, it has a crack in it," I said. Either Bob heard that joke already or my delivery was off. He might have been thinking about what his role would be in my road to recovery and was a little preoccupied. Yep, that was probably it. I'm sure Bob was second-guessing his career choice that evening.

By this time I was dilated to about a 4 so I really couldn't worry about Bob's feelings. I was thinking I could have a "C" section but Bob had a different idea. When he told me what his plan was I wasn't sure I heard him correctly. "You're going to do what while I lay here on my side," I asked. "Dang, has anyone ever survived this procedure?" He assured me that I would be OK. Well, long story short, about fifteen minutes later I hugged Bob around his neck and put him on my Christmas card list. He was truly a Godsend. When I left the hospital I felt like a new boy and yes, I had a whole face full of grin. I submit to you that I will never, never, ever, ever, ever, ever, eat trail mix while I'm on chemo again! I should add some more "nevers" to that sentence.

I hope that my story will serve as more of a public service message, if nothing else. Also, thank you to Diane for taking me to the emergency room so late that night. She was on the phone with the doctors from the Hank that entire day. Everything they called in (the meds) didn't make me deliver, so a trip to the ER was appreciated. Remember to hate the play not the player! I'll have t-shirts made up that say, "Trail Mix is Not All It's Cracked Up To Be" or "Friends don't let friends eat trail mix!" Maybe "Trail mix, the silent killer." Who knows? Anyway, I appreciate you hearing my dilemma and the fragile state I was in. It looks like I'll be OK. Amen!

Chapter Ten

Snow Day & Baby Daddy

Posted Feb 21, 2009 4:53am

Good morning everyone! Today I will officially declare a snow day. I hope to be on the couch in a few hours. Twenty-four years ago today I became a dad for the first time. The Lord blessed Diane and I with Andrew on this day in 1985. The delivery went smoothly and I made it through without any problems. Diane seemed to be pretty sweaty during the delivery and she had these huge veins in her neck that stuck out, if I remember correctly. I always heard that having a baby is pretty tough but, if you ask me, it was not a big deal. I do recall that Diane kept ramming the examination room roller table into my hospital issued recliner. I would have to wake up and rub her back. Then I would have to stop rubbing her back because I wasn't doing it right. She couldn't seem to make up her mind as to how I should rub. The ice chips I gave her became flying projectiles. Why would she throw them at me I was thinking? Man, what's a guy got to do to get a little shut-eye around here? After a while I was afraid to close my eyes. I thought she was losing her mind and could snap at any moment. I mean, it wasn't like she ate too much trail mix or something as serious as that. All in all, we both made it through.

In closing, I want to wish everyone a great weekend and hopefully we'll avoid the ten inches of snow that we're expecting. Happy Birthday Andrew! I am blessed. God bless you all in blog-land. - Jeff

Feb 21,2009- Andrew

Twenty-four years ago today I became a father for the first time with the birth of my son Andrew. Being just twenty years old myself, I really didn't know what to expect. I'm sure I was thinking this new unexpected package would change my life, and I wasn't ready for such a drastic change. Looking back, he seemed to be a strong motivating factor in my life. I was determined to do whatever it took to take care of him and to make sure I made this boy proud to call me Dad. Sometimes I would work two or three jobs to make ends meet and I was even able to get my degree in engineering. Like I say, I crammed 4 years of college into 13. Remember, I'm a little slow, and this only confirms it! Knowing this brain cancer may take me at a young age, I don't have any regrets. I feel that I have seen and done so much at an early age that I'm kind of like an old man already at 44. I've even had my 25-year wedding vows done by Elvis. What more could a boy want? Andrew has a great sense of humor and is always kind to others. I notice that he has my dad's sense of humor in him. The very same comments come out of his mouth that I can hear my dad saying.

Chapter Eleven

Christmas

Posted Feb 22, 2009 5:02am

Good morning! I woke up this morning and was very excited that the Lord has given me another day. It feels a little bit like Christmas morning, which got me thinking about Christmas as a kid. Usually, my dad would give us five or ten dollars in an envelope and take us kids to the hardware store so we could buy each other a gift. Some years we would just make each other a gift. Stacey, the youngest, would either make us a paperweight or a special art gift. The paperweight was a stone from our garden wrapped in tinfoil. The special art-type gift was usually an old car license plate that she would color in the letters with a crayon or magic marker. You can see that she is pretty artsy-craftsy. When I received these gifts I was thinking she must have pocketed the ten bucks that dad gave her. All in all, I cherish the memories from the early Christmas' and wouldn't trade them for a thing.

One year, in particular, I remember cleaning up an old pair of red, velvet platform tennis shoes that a family friend was trying to dump at the Salvation Army store. I figured with a little Brillo-pad to the white platform I could give Stacey a new pair of shoes. The only problem is that over a three-week period I created too much pre-Christmas hype and when the day came, and she finally opened my gift, she was pretty upset. She cried. Hmm. My bad!

I started this story and I wasn't sure where it was taking me but it finally came to me. I am so thankful that I have a wonderful brother and two great sisters. Looking back over all these years, I can't remember one time when one of us was mad at another. From time to time I hear people say that they haven't talked to their brother (or sister, or mom, etc) in years because they're mad at them or for some other reason. I can't understand this since I've never had to experience it. I am blessed with a great family. My brother in-law Mike fits in like a brother and my wife Diane fits in like a sister to the rest of the pack, which explains why the Vegas trip was outstanding. We did sense a little stress from Victor for a brief moment but we discounted it due to his age. I hope I delete that last sentence before I post it but, with this tumor, I might just forget! I hope not. I don't know if this short letter speaks to anyone but I would just like to say to my siblings…thanks for everything and I love you all so very much. Stacey, you can take my name off of the paperweight list this Christmas. But, I do have three old license plates that I need to get over to you!! Ann-Marie, Victor, Stacey, Diane, and Mike, I pray that you all have a blessed day and I'll see you all soon. – Jeff.
I re-read this and realize I either need my meds or I ingested too many paint chips. Oh well, I'll post it anyway.

Chapter Twelve

General Update

Posted Feb 24, 2009 7:27am

I see that Diane sent a Care page invite to my doctor at the Hank, Dr. Roy T, who has been a good source of support for me and I really appreciate him. After my last MRI, I asked him what would happen if I didn't do any more treatments. He basically reminded me that clinically I'm doing well. I'm still able to walk. I'm not having seizures. I can still see, etc. Sometimes I get a little discouraged because I'm not exactly like I used to be, but he is right. I'm very thankful for all the functions I do have and I know things could always be a whole lot worse. Sometimes I invite myself to a "Pity Party", but it's usually short-lived. I just give thanks to the Lord for everything and everyone in my life and the party usually breaks up. My objective is to be joyful always, pray a whole lot, and give thanks in every situation. (1 Thes 5:16-18). This verse always helps. I'm hopeful that this cancer can be beat.

Yesterday was a sleepy day so I didn't get anything accomplished. I had half a mind to lie around the house so my half a mind and me did just that. I was pretty worn out. More to come soon. I hope you all have a great day. - Jeff

Chapter Thirteen

New Chemo Treatment

Posted Feb 25, 2009 4:37pm

Today I started a new chemo at the Hank. My sister Stacey gave Diane a break and took me to my appointment. Thanks sis! I enjoyed the time with you. They told me that it might make me tired so I'm kind of waiting to see when. Another side effect is balding. I can't wait! Maybe I'll break out the blonde wig? I've been trying to work myself into a cowboy hat but Diane said I'm not a cowboy. "You might look goofy." she said   OK, self inventory: I'm overweight due to the steroids, my hair is thinning, my face is red and I have dry skin. Hmm, maybe the cowboy hat is not the issue… maybe it's me?? I was told to drink lots of water. I wonder if Bob the Nurse with the fat fingers called my Chemo Nurses? Lately I've been taking on more water than the Titanic! The chemo nurses threatened to put a catheter in. I couldn't find the right bathroom down the hall at the Hank and I threatened to use the corner. It was good that Stacey intervened and pointed me in the right direction. Whew!

Stacey & I had lunch and I recall that we were driving around in some parking lot again. She puts a lot of miles on her car but they're all in parking lots. We were thankful that the weather was good. It usually snows on Hank day, but not today. I was all showered and shaved when she picked me up but she did check the back of my pants to make sure I didn't have the ones with the big tear in them. On a previous trip, my undies were showing when she took me to lunch. I passed the inspection. I admit it was a pretty big rip and, of course, I couldn't keep my shirt pulled down far enough. So, it was probably pretty embarrassing. "Hey, did you see that bald, fat guy with his underwear hanging out? Quick, call the cops." Anyway, we made it back home from the Hank. Thank you for you prayers and kind words and I'll stay in touch. Have a blessed week. – Love Jeff

Chemo - The Night After

Posted Feb 26, 2009 4:59am

Yesterday, I started my first treatment of the Carbo Plattin. I don't usually look forward to my treatment day but I know it's buying me some more time. Basically, the medicine slows the tumor growth and, for right now, it's a matter of the team (the doctors) finding the right combination of medicine that works.

The day begins early since it's a 65-mile trip, one way, to the Hank. Leaving home early usually puts us on I-94 with all the crazies. I always say that everyone is "dying" to get to work.... and they drive like it. I hope I didn't' drive like that when, only a few years ago, I was doing that daily commute. But, I probably did. OK, there is the Hank campus finally. We usually hit the valet parking since it's not a whole lot more expensive than the parking deck. And, if we're nice to the chemo nurses, we can get a free parking pass from them. After the valet guy takes our car we head in and hit the elevators. We check in on whatever floor we're supposed to start on, depending on which doctor we see that day. Already, it seems like a long day!

Finally, we get ready for treatment and hit the chemo room. It's usually chilly in there so some warm blankets are always appreciated. Then, I'm assigned a good place to sit. The green vinyl recliners are nice. Next, they get me "ready to access" so they can pour in a couple bags of poison. They pour it in through an IV in the Frankenstein port in my neck. Once, Andrew asked me where it all went? Well, if I have trail mix in my system, I think it seeks it out and coagulates with it. Remember? The IV drips are usually an hour or so, which means I may get two bags that take an hour each. Two hours later we're done. I sometimes wonder if the side effects of the chemo will "do me in" during the night? But this night I survived, although I'm up early today. I slept well and my appetite is up. They say I'll lose hair, which will re-grow after I stop the chemo. But, for today, I'm the chubby guy eating in the kitchen. I'll say Amen to that!

I have to remind myself that the doctors, nurses and the people inventing the chemo are all part of God's plan to heal me. So, I have faith in that. I'll see over the next few days how I'll react to this treatment. Will I sleep a lot? Will I be sick to my stomach? I guess I'll know in a little while. That's a chemo-day in a nutshell. Some days it all goes real smoothly.

I'll give a shout-out to Stacey, Ann-Marie, Victor, Andrew, Brett, Jibber, my Cousin Scott, and Tom for taking me to a treatment or two in the past. I hope I didn't forget anyone. Thanks all! I know how much of a hassle it is, so thanks again. Also, thanks to Tom's wife Sam, Cheryl, and Wendy for getting Diane out of the house for a much needed break. And, to Mike for giving up Stacey for the day. Thanks to Stacey for the field trips and Ann-Marie for her time and lunches too. Thanks Mike for freeing up Stacey so she can enjoy treatment days. We calculated that in 2008 we put 14,000 miles on our car going back and forth to the Hank. So, when Diane can leave the house and not have to drive to Detroit I'm very grateful. OK, that pretty much sums up a treatment day. More to follow. But for now, my funny bone is taking a rest! Could it be the chemo? Right now I feel "funny" but not real funny! Does that make sense?? OK, more to follow and thanks for checking in. Have a blessed day and may God richly bless you all.

March 01

Posted Mar 1, 2009 4:30pm

OK, I'm still around! This latest chemo treatment has wiped me out. I'm not sure how many more snow days I can declare? As soon as I can get off the couch I'll check back in. All in all I'm feeling good, just tired.
Have a great day and God Bless you All. – Jeff

March 2

Posted Mar 2, 2009

Whew, they were right when they said this chemo would make me tired. At least Diane allows me to sneak a nap in whenever I want. I was just checking my email and got a chuckle. One of the subject lines was "sexy singles looking for Jeff I". Yeah, I bet they're lining up to meet the man with the moon face! I ain't single and, if you ask me, I sure ain't sexy! My eyesight is a little off but it's not that far off. Maybe the chicks in the chemo room give me a double take but I doubt it. They probably look at me and say, "Hey, I thought that guy kicked the bucket! Yep, I heard he ate too much trail mix and 'coded." Hmm, not sexy AND stupid. OK, nap time. I'll be back, good Lord willing! Thanks for all your feedback and I'll be in touch. Keep the prayers coming. Have a blessed day! - Jeff

Chapter Fourteen

You Again?

Posted Mar 6, 2009 4:34am

Diane took me in for my weekly blood work but we went to the local hospital instead of driving to Detroit. This saved us time and mileage. Why she picked the same hospital where they know me as Mr. Trail Mix I'll never know. When I was checking in the nurse said, "Oh, you've been here recently?" I said "yes, last week." She also asked me if I was a hiker? I thought yes, I'm the hiker that lies in a fetal position along the trail because I ate too much trail mix. I was hoping I didn't run into Bob the Nurse with the fat fingers on this trip. I was hoping he wouldn't recognize me. The last time I saw him I was walking like a Neanderthal (Cro-Magnon man) because I couldn't stand upright. Maybe he thought I was looking for change or checking to make sure my hiking boots were laced up? Again, a by-product of too much trail mix. Anyway, I was able to get my blood work done and get out of there without too much fanfare. So, all in all it was a good trip. And, I have been feeling good. We'll go for chemo next week. This new chemo makes me tired so I apologize for getting behind on my blogs. Have a great day and God Bless you all. - Jeff

Chapter Fifteen

Thankful

Posted Mar 7, 2009 9:17am

I'm up early again this morning praying and thinking. I am so thankful for everything. I know my days are numbered, as are all of ours, but I have no complaints. I know that my Lord has truly blessed my family and me. I really don't know how someone can go through something like cancer without trusting in God? I am thankful that I can and I am thankful for knowing each of you. I draw strength from your support. I'm thankful for my hair falling out. I save on haircuts and I don't have to waste time combing it. I'm the only one in the house with a hairy pillowcase. I'm really not thankful for my hair falling out but I accept it. Maybe that's the key? I don't see real well but I can look out of my eyes and see my wife and my boys and all the beauty that is around me. I know there are many who can't see, so I'm grateful I have what I have.

Chapter Sixteen

Stop Treatments??? Wha Huh!

Posted Mar 10, 2009 5:25pm

Diane will post the Elvis wedding pictures. They came in today! As you may have noticed, I've been a little out of pocket and not blogging too much! I'm pretty worn out. Today, I told Diane that I decided to stop my treatments! Giving up? No, but burned out. After I told her this I just didn't feel right.   This decision affects her as much as it does me. The Lord wants a husband and wife to be in agreement so we talked and prayed. At this time, we both feel it's too early to make this decision. I will continue fighting and praying for healing and God's direction as to what He wants me to do. I will continue my treatments!! Today is my kick-off day (a new day) so I will keep grinding along and seeking God's will for me in my life or, should I say, our life (Jeff &

Diane's, Andrew & Brett). I will be writing a book in hopes of helping other cancer patients and family members. Stacey will type it, Diane will proof it and check for continuity and my sons Brett & Andrew will design the cover. I will dedicate it to my Mom, as she always wanted to write one. So, here you go Barb! I ask that you keep us in prayer and, someday, we will see God's hand in this day and it will all make sense. I see the book cover. Me standing on a street holding a cardboard sign that reads... " Will Work For Chemo!" Any book comments or book titles are appreciated. Jesus loves you and so do I. - Jeff

Chapter Seventeen

Itchy Butts. And Stacey's Help!!!

Posted Mar 11, 2009 6:23pm

Today I went for treatment. The worst part is the "getting there". It's a long drive. Stacey gave Diane a break and drove me. We're both thankful for that. Since my peripheral vision is not the best I always meet new friends in the hallway at the hospital. They're the ones I "goose" as I run into them. I guess it's good that I say "I'm sorry" instead of "Hey, how you doin? You come here often?" The chemo I got today was the Avastin through my medical port that is located in my right shoulder. The nurse mentioned that my port was small and wanted to know where I had it installed? She said that most of the other men have bigger ports. At this point I'm having "port envy" so I said, "Wha?" What was she getting at? Hasn't she ever heard of port shrinkage? Hopefully

I won't run into her in the hallway! She might say "is that an undersized port in your shoulder or are you just happy to see me?"

After the treatment, Stacey & I headed for the exit to the hallway. Usually we spray our hands with sanitizer but today, for some unknown reason, Stacey sprayed a sanitizer that you use at the sink. But, she skipped the sink process. So, she slaps some in my hands and I begin to rub it in but it was more like a Mary Kay hand revitalization cream instead of sanitizer. It was exactly like putting on hand cream. The only problem now is we couldn't turn the door handles to get out to the hallway. We were prisoners of the thirteenth floor as we bounced from door to door. You remember, that's the floor all the brain cancer patients' use? So, you never know if any intelligent life will be there to help you out. The ones with brain cancer can push the elevator buttons but to ask them to open a door using the doorknob is a tall order. I was worried that we would never be found. Of course I am only kidding about the brain cancer patients. We are intelligent, just a little mixed up sometimes. In any event, we headed for water like we were ready for Noah's ark, and washed the slippery stuff off our hands. They are now useful again, thanks to the opposing thumb thing we have going on. All in all, we had a good trip and had a lot of laughs along the way.

The nurse reviewed my blood work and said I probably have the best numbers in the chemo room. But, I think she was only counting the patients who weren't fully covered by a white sheet as they were being pushed to the meat locker! Toe tags were optional on these dudes. Anywho, it was a good day and I'm continuing to pray for healing as the Lord uses these fine folks to decide my treatments and administer the dope. The Avastin has a side affect that is truly stated (here goes) "itchy anus". I read this and wondered about something. Who would report this and why? When I'm on chemo treatments they always ask if we experience anything unusual. I'm not sure I would volunteer the itchy anus issue. I might just sit tight on that one. Or, maybe I would be hollering out from my chemo recliner "Hey, this chemo is making my butt itchy!" They would probably tell me to settle down and sit still. I'm wondering if there is someone in physical therapy who would work with me and show me how to itch my butt in public without being obvious? I guess that job would stink?? I'm getting used to walking bow-legged so I guess I can break out my leather cowboy hat! I'm grateful for this day. God bless you all. I love you all. I really do. Love J.

Chapter Eighteen

Stolen Drugs

Posted Mar 12, 2009 4:34am

A few months ago my sister Stacey was telling me that there have been a few daytime break-ins at some homes in the area. The crooks would take small electronics, money and prescription medicine. With the Avastin treatment costing $12,000 a pop they won't find much money in my crib. True cost, so I'm thankful for the insurance company. But, when they say "out of pocket costs", they're talking about my pocket. I was sitting in the kitchen when Stacey told me of the break-ins so I immediately glanced to the cupboard that held my many bottles of medicine. I couldn't imagine some dude trying to make a sale on the street to some poor soul who ends up having an itchy butt, hair loss, weight gain, or being so bound up he would need to score some good stool softeners! I figured the police could easily track down the crooks if my drugs hit the street market. Instead of someone on the street corner flashing a gang signal he would be digging into his butt crack like it was on fire. The cops would be confused, I'm sure. Everyone they arrest would fall asleep in the back of the squad car complaining about needing the window cracked so they wouldn't hurl. The cops would be comparing notes with each other and realize that they are all finding a lot of hair and dry skin flakes in the back seats of the cop cars and everyone's photo mug shot would have the same peculiar moon-face. Yea, those would be the steroid junkies. "Hey, this jail jump-suit is too tight and the seat is all worn out from scratching," would echo through the jail cells. I wonder if the judge would sentence the offenders to four years or four pounds of trail mix? I think the trail mix would qualify as a death sentence. Well, I hope they catch the crooks and may the punishment fit the crime here.

The Avastin treatment seemed to go OK yesterday and I'm blessed with another day of putting my feet on the floor. I'm sure that floor will be in the kitchen since I see the dishes are piling up. Maybe I'll tell Diane I'm too tired to do dishes?? Oh, I better not. If I do she'll have me vacuuming or doing something else. I think I can handle a dirty spoon or two.

Chapter Nineteen

Deep Thoughts - by Jeff

Posted Mar 12, 2009 7:59pm

When I was first diagnosed with cancer I remember looking at the CT scan and having an immediately changed heart. Everything that I thought was important to me suddenly became unimportant and the things I thought were unimportant suddenly became important. In summary, the people in my life became so important to me and the other stuff, mostly possessions and stuff like that, became secondary. I can still remember that feeling as if were yesterday. With each new day I understand how much the Lord loves us. I look at Diane, Brett and Andrew and see them in a whole new light. The same happens when I look at my brothers Vic & Mike, and sisters Ann & Stacey. I am starting to see this when I look at my friends and extended family, too. For this, I am truly blessed.

When I look at my "special" people I get many, many tears. Diane thinks they're tumor tears but I told her I think it's the Holy Spirit. I really feel blessed. I look at Diane, tears run down my face, and then we giggle. Diane always seems to have the opposite emotion, which she calls "Nervous Energy." So, if she's laughing at the funeral, that's a good thing!! Ah man, I'm a lucky dude. The Lord has blessed me beyond measure with my Diane, my Brett and my Andrew. Lately, I always quote what Mom used to say about herself. She would say… "I'm A Mess". We all know she wasn't. She was an excellent teacher of life. She is missed. Stacey came over the other day. I looked at her and she busted me. I was crying again! She's a very special person in my life, as are Vic & Ann. God bless you all!

Chapter Twenty

Texas & Canada

Posted Mar 13, 2009 4:50am

Friday the 13th has finally arrived and we'll be heading to Houston, Texas to visit Diane's Aunt, Uncle, and cousins Davin and Beth, Diane's Mom & Dad, Uncle Roger, and sisters Donna & Darla. Sorry if I missed anyone. We'll be staying at their home. We were able to use my frequent flyer miles to get tickets so it's an inexpensive trip. If I don't purchase any trail mix at the airport that will also keep the costs to a minimum!! Diane's Uncle Dwight said I was welcome to visit but my good friend Mr. Trail Mix is not. I think he is only looking out for my best interest. The trip we took to Vegas was grueling, due to the airport shuffle, but this one should be much better since we have direct flights. We were holding off on this trip to make sure the new chemo wasn't too bad, but I really feel I should be good to go.

We'll be home on Thursday, so it's a quick trip. I'm hoping the warm weather will boost my energy level and spirits. Our friend Cheryl said that her Mom went to Florida and the warm weather is really helping her with her ailments, so this is encouraging news. Andrew and Brett will hold down the fort while we're gone. My buddies and brother have agreed to be on call in case Andrew and Brett have any problems at the house. Duane, Brother Mike, Tom, and Ken are truly appreciated. Thanks guys. Our boy Andrew offered to be our chauffeur to and from the airport. Thanks AJ. Be blessed and keep me lifted in prayer for complete healing of this tumor. Let's believe in this to happen! Amen!

Usually on Friday the 13th, some buddies and I (Bruce & Bob) ride our motorcycles to Port Dover, Canada for a big bike rally. Typically, there are several tens of thousands of bikes there from the US and Canada. But, I'll sit this one out this year. Bob just got home from heart surgery so keep him & Bev lifted in prayer for his smooth recovery too.

Funny story when I was at Port Dover last time. I was sitting on the sidewalk by my bike putting my boots on and a little boy was behind me talking to a lady. I could see them out of the corner of my eye. I was just getting ready to turn to the boy and say " Hi little fellow" but, when I turned and looked, it was a little man, not a little boy. The lady was his regular sized girlfriend. Remember in the movie Elf, when the little person beat up Buddy? That probably would have happened next, so I am glad the words never came out of my mouth! This little person had a beer in his hand, no shirt, and some six-pack abs. Since I only had one boot on at the time, he would have chased me down and probably beat me silly and stuffed me into one of my saddlebags when he caught me.

Whew, close call. I don't even think Cousin Judy from Canada would have been able to help me get back to the USA?? Note to self. Look first before speaking! I know this is Biblical in nature because, once you say something, it's hard to catch the words and cram them back in your mouth. Guard your tongue! God bless you all. – Love Jeff & Diane, Andrew & Brett!

The Chauffeur - Andrew

Posted Mar 13, 2009 6:26am

Our eldest son, Andrew arrived to take us to the airport this morning. I heard the garage service door jiggle so I went over to unlock it. I asked through the closed door, "Who is it?" Andrew said, " It's me." I opened the door and he said, "Don't worry, I'm not here to steal your medicine!!" Ha Ha. OK, he's checking the blogs!! So, we'll talk to you all soon. God bless.
Jeff & Diane

Texas Trip!!

Posted Mar 19, 2009 8:33am

Welcome to the first day of spring! Flurries expected here. I guess I'll declare a snow day and hit the couch! Well, Diane and I made it home from Houston. We went there to visit her Aunt & Uncles and cousins. Her sisters, nephew, and Mom and Dad were there too. I enjoyed seeing everyone, but I think I ruined the trip. The airport shuffle was pretty tiring on me. Diane's sister, nephew, and mom ended up with the flu (or something) so that put me into a panic mode as I turned into a germ-freak… green mask and all. Which, by the way, Roger found very amusing. Roger, Diane's Uncle, is mentally disabled and he smiles all the time. But it's rare to hear him laugh and, when he looked at me with the goofy green mask, he got a good chuckle. So, I'm glad someone enjoyed the mask. I probably looked and acted like an escapee from the nut house. In the old days I never worried about getting sick. But, since the cancer, I'm just tired of always feeling "not well." If I can avoid getting sick, that means I can avoid more medicine and doctor's visits.

Aunt Diane & Uncle Dwight's home was awesome. It had lots of space and was situated on the lake. It was great to see Beth, Ryan, Davin, Sheila, (and Lucy the dog) but I won't try to name the cats. It was nice to see Uncle Roger too.

Well, we flew home a day early and I feel just terrible about that. I feel I cut into Diane's vacation time with her family. We did agree, however, that this would be our last trip like this, at least until I'm healed. As I mentioned earlier, I am pretty discouraged. The reason for that is I struggled through the traveling. In the old days, I traveled so much that it was never a problem. But, these days it's exhausting. I have to rely on Diane so much. I do remind myself that I am grateful for what I can do. I'm not in a wheel chair so I can still get around. And, even though I don't see well, I can at least still see. Peripheral vision is gone but I can see OK looking forward. I do thank God everyday for what I have and what I can do. I'm hopeful I'll return to my old self. I say, "Who knows?" but I know God knows if it's meant to be.

When we got to Detroit, I was glad to see our boys (Brett & Andrew) pull up to pick us up. Maybe someday I'll get back to Houston on my Harley? It's possible! Through Jesus Christ all things are possible. I guess we only need to be invited back to Houston. I think Diane will get an invite, but she might have to leave freaky-J back home!! As I tell Diane, I'm a mess! Ha, ha, ha. I'm not giving up! I haven't heard if everyone is feeling better yet but I'm hopeful they are. Being on vacation and not feeling well is not enjoyable. Plus, they have to get back home to Tennessee. A quick thanks to my buddies & brother-in-law who agreed to be on-call in case the boys had any problems at the house with the well, furnace, etc. Thanks Ken, Duane, Mike, and Tom. Thankfully all was well. Thank you Uncle Dwight & Aunt Diane for you hospitality and for the airport size of hand sanitizer. God bless you. - Jeff

March 19, 2009

Hi all. I was able to squeeze in a few naps and peek at the Care pages and am overwhelmed by the love and support from every one of you. It was nice to see my co-workers chime in, as I miss them all so very much. I was glad to see my cousins, friends, and brother and sisters. I miss you too!! I'm hoping after a couple days of rest I will get blog-busy again. It's a great outlet for me because I seem to only be able to blow off stress through laughter. Between my faith in God and laughter, I'm able to plug along. I'm planning on starting my book within the next couple of days. It will be something that Mom always wanted to do but was unable to. So, I'll do it for her by proxy. I was able to see the need for it today because a sister in-law of Diane's friend may have the same type of cancer that I have. And, I know that if it is, the road they have before them will be tough. So, if I can collect some helpful thoughts and humor to help them navigate the bumpy road, there may be some value to the book. I pray there will be. – Jeff.

Chapter Twenty One

Dr. Roy & my Hank visit today!!

Posted Mar 20, 2009 5:36pm

My March 20, 2009 hospital visit went well today. I got a hug from my doctor and I punched a nurse. The punch happened as I was taking my coat off and she was standing on my left side, which is the side I'm lacking my peripheral vision. I didn't see her and accidentally bumped her hip, twice! I think she'll be OK. The hug from Dr. Roy was just an added bonus. Maybe he was checking to make sure I had my wallet? Diane has a photo that she posted of Dr. Roy and me. Dr. Roy and I had a good discussion regarding our faith in God. I told him that I don't know how anyone can go through this without faith and humor and he commented that his patients with faith do much better than those without. After learning he's a man of God it felt like a ton of bricks fell off my shoulders. I know he and Jesus have my back! With that combination, I feel pretty good! No CT (cat scan) was scheduled and we'll do an MRI after my next treatment of chemo. The doctor's think the smells I'm experiencing are seizures, so they upped my meds and we'll just monitor it. I get chills and then I smell weird smells, which may be seizures. I'm wondering if a bar of soap and a good shower might fix my smelly problem? The guy in the elevator suggested that! Hmm, I didn't catch what floor he got off on, probably some rectal-related floor? Dr. Roy asked Diane if I really ate that much trail mix? I tried to down play it but she threw me under the bus. He looked happy that Nurse Bob attended to me and not him!! I did show him how I had to sit sidesaddle in the car on the way to the emergency room to see Nurse Bob (with the big fingers)! After my demonstration, I know he was glad I went to see Bob and not him!

I'll continue with the Carbo Platt chemo. I told Dr. Roy, "It's great, but it makes my butt-itchy." Usually, the good doctor will throw a script at me to counteract any problems I'm having but, for some odd reason, he didn't offer me anything for the itchy butt.

All in all, we had a good visit to the Hank. But, as always, glad to be home. God is good, all the time! Bless you all and I'll blog at you later. Thanks for the prayers, as I'll keep all of you in prayer too! Love Jeff.

When?

Posted March 21, 2009

One of the consuming aspects of this disease for me is trying to figure out when and how this brain cancer first entered my body. I sometimes will say, "I sure didn't sign up for it." I probably would have picked something like halitosis. Which by the way was one of the outward signs before my diagnosis. As soon as I began radiation the bad breath went away. One of the patients I was talking with the other day had just the opposite effect. His name was Buzz. As soon as he started radiation he started having bad breath. So, between him and me, we were some pretty popular guys in the waiting room. We never seemed to have any trouble finding a good seat when we went for treatment. I'm sure when we talked to someone it felt like they just got hit in the face with a brick. Maybe that's why they called me butt-breath? I'm now thinking that the trail mix might have countered this horrible condition?

Another sign of this disease in its early stage was rational reasoning. I was thinking that Diane was going crazy. But she insisted it was me that was going crazy. There was no way I could accept that it was me. But looking back, I can see she was right. Another outward sign was fatigue, which I dismissed as "just me getting older." I had a hard time completing anything on my daily to do list. I have always tried to keep busy and always seemed to have several projects going. But it just seemed I could never get anything done, which was frustrating. I thought I was having sinus problems. But, it's pretty clear to me now that it wasn't.

Diane said I was ditzy! With my vast knowledge of medical terminology I don't think ditzy is one they have in the books, but it does paint a pretty clear picture of my previous mental status. I recall a good example of ditzy. The day I went out of work I remember that my company's vice president walked by my desk and, as I spun my chair around, I said "Hi Jeff." I thought I must have looked pretty cool. But then he stopped and said "no, you're Jeff." Then it dawned on me that his name was Mark. He was probably trying to figure out who hired idiot-boy.

In summary, I'm not saying sinus issues and fatigue are sure signs of brain cancer. So don't read too much into it, unless you have some really foul breath. OK, just kidding!! A few breath mints and you'll be on your way to a full recovery. Yeah, don't think that some bad breath is a sign of cancer either. ☺.

The bottom line is that I just can't place my finger on a particular time or event that I can say, "Ah ha, that was when the cancer started." I just have to come to terms that it just happened and not get all caught up in it. Dwelling on it just wastes precious energy and serve no good purpose. So, if I find myself festering in trying to figure out when and how it all started, I just push past it and realize it does me no good. So, don't sweat it!

Chapter Twenty Two

PMS and Medical Language

Posted Mar 21, 2009 3:47am

Learning the medical lingo! During my illness with cancer, Diane and I have spent countless hours at the hospital and doctor's office while receiving treatments and being evaluated. So, of course, we begin to pick up the medical terminology that is used such as scripts, meds and so on. I also realized that there are just some medical conditions that don't have fancy words. Trail mix is still plain old trail mix but a digital exam isn't as high-tech as it sounds. Especially when Nurse Bob is in the room!

Yesterday, Diane explained to Dr. Roy that I have been crying a lot. I can pretty much turn on the waterworks at the drop of a hat. They are not tears of sadness, but of joy. Sometimes I won't even start a sentence when someone asks me something because I know I'll be crying too hard to even finish it. So, I just smirk and cry. Diane was thinking it was tumor related so she asked Dr. Roy what was going on with me? As he began to explain something about highs and lows and some other stuff I thought boy, they're going to have to rush me to a special wing at the hospital that may include a Life-flight Team. I must be in rough shape but I still couldn't extract the medical term for my condition. So, I looked at him and said, "I don't think I understand?" Next, he looked at me and said, "You have PMS." This I knew as a survivable condition so I felt much better. Maybe it's caused by the fact that I carry a man-bag, also known as a "murse", when I leave the house? Where else would I carry my tampons and lip-gloss? The bottom line is this disease puts my emotions in a raw state, so they pop up easily. OK, I can live with that, although I'll need to learn the medical term for it so I can impress my friends and family with my in-depth medical knowledge.

I'm trying to use this newly found magic to my advantage. When Diane asks me to fold laundry I just stand there and cry. Maybe this PMS will actually be a helpful tool and not a problem? I've been wishing for a recliner chair. Maybe Diane and I could go to the furniture store to look for one. When the salesperson tells me the price I could just start crying. "That's too expensive." Hmm, this PMS thing has a lot of possibilities. I wonder if Diane has any practical applications for it? I'll have to ask her.

Well, I'm thanking the Lord for another day and I appreciate all of your prayers and words of encouragement. I see your blog feedback and hope to be able to respond to them all. May God bless you all, as He has my family and me. Thank you – Jeff.

Chapter Twenty Three

Still Blaming the Sinuses!

Yesterday morning I had a headache when I woke up but nothing a Tylenol couldn't fix. It made me think of my older sister, Ann-Marie, who has migraines every so often. I'll have to check in with her today to see how she's doing. As Diane was getting my pills, I told her I thought my headache was sinus related. I usually have sinus problems during March, April, and May every year. I would probably have been a good company-man at a lumberjack camp. "Hey Jeff, do you think your headache is due to that axe handle sticking out of your head?" "Huh? Oh no, I don't think so. It's probably just this damp weather." Anyway, the headache went away as fast as it came so I think I'll be fine. Amen! Diane mentioned that I had a tumor and said maybe the headache was related to that. But, that sure doesn't make sense to me. I'd rather blame it on the weather. Yes, I know, I'm an extremely slow learner. Maybe blaming it on my sinuses is a defense mechanism but, whatever it is, I got through it without much fanfare. I guess that's the name of the game at this point!

This cancer road is always filled with curves so I'm learning to bend and adjust. If you don't bend a little you might break. So, try not to get too locked in. Stay on your toes because everyday is a new adventure with a new set of obstacles. If you over-do it on the trail mix, staying on your toes will be virtually impossible and, there will be no way you can bend with the road. I think I'm becoming the poster-child for the anti-trail mix community. I'll need to get a couple pictures of my face on a poster that says, "This is Jeff" and then another that says "This is Jeff on Trail mix". I think you know this campaign and the rest of the story.

New prescription – Fireproof

Posted March 22, 209

While talking with Dr. Roy the other day, he mentioned a movie called Fireproof. I told him that my sister Stacey bought it so we'll check it out. Diane and I watched it the other night. I'm glad that Dr. Roy just told me about the movie and didn't write a prescription (a.k.a., Script) for the movie. My out of pocket insurance costs would probably have been about $11,089.00. So, I guess I got off cheap on this one. It was good medicine and I think you can buy the movie at the Christian bookstore.

As I was lying in bed this morning I was thinking about my church. But, I don't think I will be attending today. I'm still a little concerned about catching a cold or flu. I can hear everyone coughing, sniffling, sneezing, and then shaking hands and hugging each other. I'm not sure I can deal with that today. I love and miss my church family but I may sit this day out. But, I know they still have me in their prayers and thoughts.

Enjoy the day!

Verse of the day – 1 Thessalonians 5:16-18

Have a blessed day!

Love Jeff.

Chapter Twenty Four

Germs and the Body-condom

March 23, 2009 – Germ In Town:

My dad was a big fan of Roger Whittaker and I can remember one of Roger's songs called German-town. But, the town I'm stuck in is spelled "Germ In-Town" and I'm trying to catch the next train out before Diane and the boys have me committed to the nut house. Yep, I've officially become a heavy-duty germ freak. Since I've never been one, Diane is blaming it on the tumor. She said, "The way you're acting, the tumor must be the size of a football." The best thing about Diane is that throughout our twenty-five year marriage I never had to worry about what she's really thinking, because she'll tell me. And, I don't even need to ask! As a defense mechanism over the years I've always tried to avoid the phrase "what's wrong?" I'm a firm believer that if you ask, you probably already know the answer. Playing dumb will last only so long but, in my case, it was nearly three decades.

Jeff, the freaky germ-boy, probably needs to be put on the germ-free bus, told not to touch anything, and sent away.

That would be fine as long as that place wasn't called Bacteria Bayou, New Mucus Junction, or Snotsville.

Anyone who knows me would agree that I'm always trying to come up with the next multi-million dollar idea. So, I'm thinking this may be a good time to introduce the new and improved Body Condom with the patented germ-jelly. When someone stops by the house for a visit I could ask them "did you bring any protection?" This idea could keep me safe and germ-free for life! I have some details to work out first. Would the body condom be colored, clear or opaque? How would I incorporate armholes? Would there be a cell phone pocket so someone could practice "safe-text"? Would one-size fit most? Would it have to have ribs? Could they hand them out in schools? If my mom found it, would she believe it was a cover for my snowboard or the new ironing board cozy I was getting her for Christmas?

OK – I need to draw up sketches of the new body-condom and hopefully I'll be germ-free going forward. I kind of realized that I had become a germ-freak when Diane's Aunt Diane gave me an airplane-sized bottle of hand sanitizer when we left their home in Texas last week. If you recall, Diane's family was ill during our visit to Houston so I was running around in my green mask, like a nut-job, in hopes of avoiding germs. Too bad I didn't have a body condom! Maybe for our next trip! So, if you stop in for a visit and I chase you around with a can of anti-bacterial spray or watch your every move like an eagle, try not to take offense. Our sons will remind me that if I can't find them they'll be in the kitchen coughing on the doorknobs. So this, no doubt, brings me more comfort as they slowly push me over the edge! Man, maybe I should have been nicer to them in their younger years? :)) I plan to survive this germ-thing.

Chapter Twenty Five

Growing Up or Growing Old?

Posted Mar 25, 2009 5:30am

As Diane and I were driving back from an appointment we passed what appeared to be a retired couple. My PMS kicked in and I began to tear up. I couldn't help thinking that this cancer may prevent us from enjoying the leisurely life of travel and enjoying each other's company, as we grow older. I then began to think that it's not over yet and it's possible that we will be spending a lot of time together. Through prayer, I'm still remaining hopeful that the perfect combination of treatments will cure this brain tumor and life will go on. It also dawned on me that by the time we reach retirement age, she might be so tired of me that traveling with me would not be an option anyway. She would not have enough energy to carry the diaper bag. This leads me to my next topic, which is about the physical changes associated with being diagnosed with a heavy-duty illness. And, the challenges we will face. It isn't pretty, but I'll explain (as you knew I would!)

As I've told my kids, I may be the guy shuffling around the house eating apple sauce so be prepared. And, always expect the unexpected. I've got the shuffle thing down to a science but Diane is throwing so much yogurt at me that I haven't had time for applesauce. I think she feels that yogurt will counteract any side affects of trail mix in the unlikely event I do some weekend binge crunching, like a party-starved frat-boy! For now, whatever she's feeding me seems to be working. Not to mention the gallons of water I seem to be drinking on a daily basis. I guess when I said, "Hey, this trail mix is making me thirsty," it didn't fall on deaf ears (unless I was talking to my brother, Victor). In that case, I'd be spooning Nurse Bob on the green gurney getting reacquainted at the ER. I did, however, help him rename some hospital equipment. I kept referring to the wheel chair with the commode as the "Superbowl chair". When his puzzled look indicated to me that he didn't understand, I said, "I need to get a chair like that for the big game." I wouldn't have to interrupt the game for a potty break, and I could remain seated while I roll myself into the kitchen for some more of that magical mix that I've come to know and love. Also, the super bowl chair is fitted with a nice little table so I could monitor my wagers. Anyway, it seemed like a better invention than the body condom and probably a lot more marketable. I guess time will tell.

OK, getting back to growing. Now, I'm not sure if I'm growing up or growing down. I think I would say that growing up is growing old and growing down is heading for the days when I first emerged from the womb. As of right now, my sleep patterns are all jacked up so I am feeling more like a child or someone that is growing down. As I shuffle around the house I began to see things that we used to purchase when the kids were babies. Why is Diane insisting that we continue to buy the same things? I'm seeing the familiar butt-wipes, ointments, creams, and salves that always seemed to eat into our grocery budget but were the required tools for every diaper bag we carried. Today I don't carry a diaper bag but a Murse, as my niece Morgan calls it. A murse is a glorified name for a man-purse. I carry one so I can conceal my wipes, medicine, and any special salves I may need on that particular day. Ok, so it's a glorified diaper bag, even if I try to pretend I'm lugging around my laptop. During the airport "bag-drag" reroute to Houston, the TSA guys kept telling me to remove my laptop before I laid my bag on the belt. I had to keep revealing the fact that there is no laptop in it. I probably could have saved a lot of time by telling them it was my diaper bag. But, I'm thinking that the x-ray scanner told them this already.

I'm continuing to receive more lessons in humility as I have to use the baby wipes more often, or holler from the bathroom, "Hey honey, do we have anymore A&D ointment?" This A&D ointment is confusing to me. First of all, do I put this grease on my A or my D? I'm not sure, but I wonder who came up with that name? Was it a boardroom joke that got out of hand? Weird, I think!

In closing, I am thankful that there is a countermeasure for whatever grim joke this chemo can play. I'll just have to make sure my diaper bag is well equipped, as I do know that things could always be a lot worse. We'll be leaving for another treatment so I had better get packing my murse. Let's see, I need to make sure I pack the hand sanitizer or "Hanny – Sanny" as we now refer to it. I think this cute new name minimizes the fact that freaky J is a bona-fide nut case when it comes to germ warfare. If you hear a rattle in my murse it's probably a case of tic-tacs. But then again, maybe I'll need to dig deeper into the bag and see if Diane is playing some cruel joke on me? Hopefully I won't find a burp-rag! However, in the right situation, it may come in handy.

May the Lord bless your day and remind us all to be thankful for all that we have and for all that we are still able to do. God bless you all – Jeff.

Chapter Twenty Six

My Faith

Posted Mar 26, 2009 3:08am

My faith: This topic is one that I've been looking forward to sharing with you all. As I've mentioned earlier, it's been something that I've been able to draw upon for strength as I move down this road with a head full of cancer. During our trip to visit Diane's Aunt and Uncle in Houston, I woke up early one morning to the voice of a T.V. Evangelist. He was preaching up a storm. As I listened, I was thinking that his message and enthusiasm was strong but I felt that, to some listeners, he might be actually turning them off. Thus, the seed was planted as to how I would explain my faith to others. I've shared it with others but wasn't sure I could put it on paper. So, here it goes.

As a boy, my mother made sure we attended church on a weekly basis. I had the knowledge of who God was. They must have seen that I had some religious potential because I was given some sanctuary clothes and a job title. Yeah, they called me an altar boy. I was hauling crosses down the aisle, ringing bells, holding Bibles, and doing all kinds of things to keep busy. My Mom's brother, Uncle Bill, was a Roadie for a Detroit rock band. Maybe this Altar-boy training would have been a good stepping-stone for me to become a Roadie for Jesus. My Uncle's downfall was when he tried to park the band's 12-foot tall truck under an 8-foot awning and nearly went through the windshield. I'm not sure I have the whole story but I 'm guessing some mind-altering substances may have been used before he got behind the wheel. But, that would be pure speculation on my part so I'll leave it there. With his long hair, I did think of him as a Hippie. But, he would always call it musician's hair. Maybe his musician's hair was in his eyes when he sandwiched the truck or maybe he just needed some Altar-boy training? I'm guessing that either one would have worked. I'm still curious as to how my Dad allowed him to move in with us on the farm. But, looking back, it was actually a good idea. And, I'm a better person today for that decision made way back in 1975.

My earlier religious exposure was belonging to a Religion and trying to stay within the boundaries. At the ripe old age of twenty I married my high school girlfriend, Diane. Yes, she is the same Diane I've been married to all these years later. Once her Father unloaded the shotgun we began a new chapter in our lives. Diane grew up with the Baptist influence of her family and I was brought up in the Catholic faith. So, we fit together like a Braille jigsaw puzzle. I would eventually try different traditional religions in hopes of finding one that we could both agree on. We both knew it was important that our boys have some type of religious influence.

In 1989 I took a job in Nashville, Tennessee. I moved an apartment full of furniture, two cars, a motorcycle, a toddler, and a pregnant wife 700 miles to begin our new life. The ironic part is that our new neighbors were Christians and my new buddy Jeff was one of those guys who worked for the organization that places Bibles in the Flamingo-type Motel night stands. You know, the hotel rooms that a CSI unit would be afraid to enter without a bottle of Luminal, a black light and a body condom? You never know what will jump on you from the bedspread or the shower curtain. To this day, Diane and I are still very close to Jeff & Shelly, even after all these years and miles that are between us. After 8 years in the South, I started a new job and was asked to relocate to Michigan. So, we made the trip back North. It was nice to be back home!

In 1998 Diane's brother completed suicide and the devastation was immense. During this time, Diane had submitted that she would get to know this Jesus and place her trust in Him. In the days and weeks following her decision she would continually approach me, Bible in hand, and say, "Hey, listen to this." Or, "You need to read this." Each time I saw her coming at me with the Good Book I'd say, "Oh no, here comes freaky D." She wasn't off the deep end yet but she sure seemed to have a good view of it, or so I thought. Yeah, I thought she was a certified nut-bag and I needed my space. I didn't need to be pestered by this Jesus lady, a new card carrying member of the God Squad. But over time, I began to see a strength that was building in her and she was able to help her family members cope with the devastation that surrounds a family during that extremely difficult time. I took notice and decided that I would look into this religious stuff for myself.

I attended a youth rally with our church and the overriding theme that weekend was 'Jesus doesn't want you to change but he wants you to come to Him.' So, in May of 2007

I made the decision to learn about this Jesus guy. From that day forward I was able to build my relationship with Him. My faith is not based on a religion but on a relationship with Jesus Christ. I don't know how I, or anyone, could navigate this cancerous road without being able to rely on Christ and the hope of heaven that awaits me.

I even took some training courses and became a Chaplain. Being a chaplain didn't make me more religious or stronger in my faith but it did give me the credentials to start a Bible-study at our local, minimum-security jail. I'm sure when they saw me coming they thought, "Oh no, here comes that Bible thumping freaky J. What a nut-bag."

That pretty much sums up my testimony. The thing I would really like to stress is this. Knowing God is based on my relationship with Him and not a religious thing. I'm far from perfect and will never be close to perfect but I lean upon this scripture verse on a daily basis. Be joyful always, pray continually, and give thanks in all circumstances, for this is God's will for you through Christ Jesus. Praying continually does not mean staying on my knees 24-7 but just having a continual dialog with God. So, if my lips are moving I may be praying or, it may be the football-sized tumor in my head. More than likely, it's me praying. So, don't freak-out and think that I'm possessed! J.

Chapter Twenty Seven

Lesson Learned

March 27 2009

On Wednesday, Diane and I were heading to the Hank for my scheduled chemo treatment and it started out as "one of those days." You know, the kind of day you could probably do without. Like Trail Mix without the little chocolate pieces, but a whole lot of it with the nuts that seem to grow some type of gray fuzz. Well, we were up to our necks in fuzz that morning and we weren't wearing dickeys. By the way, who designed the dickey? Is it a neck warmer / turtleneck and will this freak-of-fashion ever make a comeback? I guess this question will find itself in my next conversation with Victor. I'm still waiting to find out if the denim jumpsuit will reappear on the racks at my local Gap store. Hmm, we'll see. Well, getting back to treatment day. I can easily set up the tone by saying it was a cold, wet morning and a few more hours in the crib would have helped. But, when you have a schedule to keep, you just try and push on. Looking back, the lessons I learned came from a whole host of people including Andrew, Brett, my brother in-law Mike, Diane, my mother, and my high school buddy Jim.

That morning I was pretty tired and was going to tell Diane that I wanted to cancel my treatment and just stay home. With the chemo being my life sustaining option it didn't seem like a good decision. So, I continued to finish my shower. As I was getting dressed I remembered the days that I would take care of my mom. I would have to get her dressed because the M.S would not allow her to do it by herself. Immediately, I was thankful that I was still able to care for myself, and suddenly getting ready for the day didn't seem so bad. So, I pushed on with a new sense of gratitude.

Around 9:09 a.m., Diane and I headed out to the garage to begin our pre- travel ritual as we got ready for our trip to Detroit. The ritual is usually the same. We open the car doors and I spin in circles naming off things that we need to take and she slides into the driver's seat. As I continue to spin in circles I say, "Purse, coffee, calendar, jacket, medicine, bottle of water, cell phone? Do we have gas? Hey, where's my murse? I need my murse. Have you seen my murse? Do you have your purse? How about your wallet? Is it in your purse?" Diane replies, "You're gonna drive me to drink!" Anyway, we eventually back out of the garage, probably forgetting something in spite of my pre-trip reconnaissance. But, this morning, we were ready to roll (or so we thought).

A few miles after we pulled out of our driveway we heard what sounded like a flat tire. I say it sounded like a flat tire because that's exactly what it was, flat! The old Jeff would have jumped out of the car, slung on a new tire, and we would have been on our way. But, the "new" Jeff knew that with two brain surgeries and an itchy butt he probably couldn't tackle this task. And, Diane would not have let me anyway. So, it was just another reminder of some of the independence I have lost. I asked Diane to pull over and I would take a look and see if we really had a flat tire. As I looked at the tire my PMS flared up and I began to cry. "Yep it's flat!" Diane said, "Do we have a jack and a spare?" I said yes, but could you hand me a tissue? Well, with the chemo tears flowing down my cheeks I knew I was not going to be the selected candidate for this tire change. As usual, Diane would fix this dilemma. She called our son Brett, who woke up his brother Andrew, and the problem would soon be solved.

In the Bible there's a scripture verse that says, "Do everything without complaining," and that was my lesson for the day. As the boys pulled up they sprung into action. They traded cars with us and let me know that they had my back. The weather was a cold and windy mist, but it didn't slow them down. We left them on the roadside to fix the tire. Since Brett had to be in court for a traffic ticket and Andrew was adjusting from his work swing-shift schedule, I figured that there might be a chance that they would have been griping about their newly arranged morning, but they didn't. As we were driving I was reminded of the scripture that tells us to do everything without complaining. I was thankful for the lesson they gave me that morning and was extremely proud of the character they displayed. Amen

By the end of the day my mechanic, and high school buddy, Jim had set us up with a new tire and the boys got it mounted. My brother-in-law Mike, Stacey's husband, caught wind of our morning tire problem and told Diane that we could have called him. He's another one who is always ready to jump in and help without complaining. Hmm, I think I'm catching on! That evening I was telling the boys that I appreciated my lessons that day. Brett even wore a suit to court and looked good when he got home. So, it was a good day all around. Man, am I blessed?

That evening I was telling Brett that I could be saying, "Oh man, I have brain cancer" and come up with a list of complaints as thick as my college transcripts. But, that would only waste time and energy and not do one thing to help me. I told him that eighty percent of the people you know don't want to hear your problems and the other twenty percent are glad you have them! So, don't be a complainer and try to focus on the possible solutions to your problems. Brett said, "OK Dad, I got it! Save the lecture." Yeah, I got it too. Thanks! And thanks to Andrew, Diane, Brett, Mom, Mike, and Jim. I hope the next lesson will require less people. Jim did get an extra bonus…he was able to see how I can cry at the drop of a hat. Maybe that's why he gave us a good deal on the tire? I told him I could come over and shuffle around his shop but he told me he'd take a rain check on that one. He felt I was too much of a liability around all his expensive tools and equipment. He's probably right. Knowing me, I'd probably end up facedown in the grease rack. Hey, I wonder if he would give me a lube job if I brought my A & D ointment over? Knowing Jim, probably not. But, I could always ask. In the end, the Lord blessed our day. Philippians 2:14

Chapter Twenty Eight

A Typical Treatment Day

Mar 27, 2009

The word treatment has become a normal word around our home and has become a big part of all of our lives. Treatment is receiving chemo and it's a necessary disruption on this cancerous road in hopes of a full recovery. After the treatments I usually feel like I jumped onto the wrong road, along with my fatigue and my itchy butt. Just getting to and from the hospital is exhausting enough. But cram a few bags of chemo, minus the trail mix, into your veins and it's a whole new game. Most treatment days are the same. But, since we live sixty-five miles away, we always have to deal with the weather and the traffic. That seems to be the price we pay to live in the country instead of the city. I have a good support team that helps get me to my treatments. Diane usually takes me. However, Stacey, Ann-Marie or my friend Jibs is always ready and able to jump in and take me. I mean, who wouldn't want to waste a whole day sitting in a hospital after dealing with a snowstorm and all the bad drivers on the freeway?

If there were such a thing as a typical treatment day it would look something like this. It usually starts with me encountering some self-induced stress as I'm sitting in the passenger's seat. I've done the Detroit commute most of my life and I'm sitting there wishing I was driving. But, considering my poor eyesight, I don't seem to be anyone's first choice to put behind the wheel. I miss the old days but I'm hopeful I'll be driving again. I'm sure I used to complain about having to make that commute to work. Maybe I just need to sit back, shut up, and relax. Hey, those are the words that Stacey told me a few moths ago while she was taking me to one of my treatments. I told her "turn around because I'm not going today!" But, after her three or four hour investment in me that morning, she basically let me know that she was driving the bus and the plan was that I was going. That was pretty much the end of that exchange. So, we pushed on.

My plan change reminded me of a story my Dad told me once. He told me that when I was in Kindergarten he got a call from my teacher one day. She asked my Dad if we were moving out of town or changing schools. Of course, my dad replied "No, why?" "Well", she said, "Jeff told me not to order him anymore milk because he wouldn't be coming back." True story. Dad made sure I made it back. Looking back, 'free milk and a daily nap, why wouldn't I want to go back? I'm guessing a bad day in Kindergarten beats a good day at treatment anytime!

One of the decision points on the way to treatment is whether we park in the deck or use the hospital valet service. The whole valet process always causes me a little stress. As we pull into the staging lane I go into a hyper-scan mode of the car's cabin. I'm looking for anything that these car-jockeys could steal. I observe 2 dimes and a penny in the cup holder and immediately think that this will end up being some form of economic stimulus for the guy in the red jacket. Who, by the way, now has possession of the keys. Oh yeah, he'll be laughing at us later as he's dropping some change on a pack of smokes at the local liquor store. Dang, they'll make a fool of me again. "Whose phone number is on this piece of paper in the door pocket?" Quick, I'd better grab it and put it in my pocket. I'm pretty confident that the red coats will be crank-calling this number at midnight as they're puffing on their smokes. Oh no, they might spit in my Hanny Sanny. Dang, here they come. I'm trapped. Quick, get me out! My only options are to try and scoop up some more of their 'potential booty' or make the twenty-yard dash to the hospital's lobby. I guess I'll meet you in the lobby I tell my driver of the day.

As I reach for the lobby door, I can't help thinking how many sick people have already touched the automatic door switch that morning. A quick tap with my elbow will hopefully get me inside without touching any more germs. Note to self, get my jacket dry-cleaned and have them double up on the elbow area. OK, let's head to the elevators. Maybe I can hit the call button with the previously violated elbow of my jacket. It's either that or do the bum-rush into the box- o-funk when the doors open. Man, when the elevator door opens, you never know who's in there just waiting to infect you with some other ailment that might not even be related to cancer. Hey, do you have any Mersa I can get from you? OK, I'll wait here.

While riding up to the 13th floor I try to hold my breath. These folks in here look pretty sick. I'll just stand over here next to the dude with the yellow skin tone. He looks greasy and smells like A & D ointment but he seems to be my safest choice for an elevator-buddy. When the button with a 13 on it finally lights up I bolt from my tomb of terror, leaving Jaundice Johnny behind. I head quickly for the nearest hand sanitation station. Whew, what a morning I've had already. Bring on the chemo!

After I check in at the desk one of the chemo nurses appears and greets me with a "Hi Jeff" and then takes me to the chemo room. OK, let's get this party started, I'm thinking. They take me to another room and get me hooked up with an IV line. Since I have a medi-port they don't have to do a conventional IV, but they do what they call "accessing my port." I think many marriages have broken up because the man had his port accessed. But, this application is different and pretty simple. I have a little tube under my skin on the right side of my chest that is used to main line the chemo directly into my vein. I guess it looks like an inverted shoulder nipple.

Next, I'm taken to one of several green vinyl recliners and given a pillow and blanket. The nurse checks my paperwork and puts a medical bracelet on me. Then, a couple bags of chemo, which I affectionately refer to as poison, are hung on the IV pole. Then the fun begins. In a couple of hours I'll be done and ready to head home. This means I'll have to run back through the gauntlet, between the hand sanitation station on the thirteenth floor and the guy with my car keys. Except this time, I'll have an itchy butt and nausea to make the trek a little more challenging. All this courtesy of the two bags of chemo and it's accompanying side affects. All right, good times!

In closing, the trip to treatment is never easy. But, the wonderful nurses in the chemo room do a great job taking care of me. They always have a smile on their faces and a kind word. I love them all and I'm thankful that they're on my team. May the Lord bless them and their families, as I know they have a tough job. Diane, my family and I are grateful to call them friends.

Chapter Twenty Nine

Getting the Day Started

Apr 1, 2009

Well, as you guessed it, it's me. I am thankful to put my feet on the floor one more time. It's almost 2:30 A.M. I know it's early. I bet most people who are up at this hour are looking for a last call bar somewhere. But, here I am trying to decide whether or not I should have some peanut butter toast. I decided on the toast. I'm trying to be quiet out here in the kitchen since everyone else is sleeping. But, when I push the toaster button down it makes a nasty buzzing sound. Who designed this buzzer? It's worse than dragging my fingernails on the proverbial chalkboard. I'm thinking that my whole day may be like this. Well, it could be worse.

Anyway, what's my day going to look like? Stacey will be taking me on a field trip so this will give Diane a break. I have to go to a hospital in a neighboring town to do some blood work in preparation of my next chemo treatment. I hope I make it there before last call. I think they may be having a special on two-for-one chemo. Well drinks only. I love the little bowls of trail mix they set out. I'll hide my Hanny-Sanny in my pocket because who knows how many urine soaked fingers I'll be sharing the trail mix with? Dang, it seems like everything revolves around germs! It's got to be this crazy tumor talking? Bring on happy hour because this tumor is making me thirsty. OK, here's a recap: Up early; blood work today; toaster buzzer screwed up my morning; feet on the floor. But, I'm thankful for another day!! Yes, that's the main thing.

I see that Andrew left his widow-makers at the top of the stairs again. I asked him to move them last night. Of course he asked, "What are widow-makers?" I said, "Your shoes. If I trip on them and fall down the stairs your mom is going to be a widow a lot quicker than she expected." Anyway, I've learned to watch out for them so I think I'll be o.k. I'm not looking forward to kicking the bucket because I think it will be a lot harder on the ones left behind. I'll miss my Diane. Oh crap, PMS alert. Quick, think of the bacteria on the doorknob or the toilet seat. Oh yeah, that toilet seat. I'm hoping that 20/20 doesn't do an expose on it. I'll tell you right now, I couldn't handle it. Do they make a booty-sanny? Hmm, a potential supplement to the body condom. Another one of my great ideas. I could make it scented and call it the Fruity Booty Spray. OK, I'll work on it. I'm just trying to avoid any booty cooties because the "building a nest" thing seems flawed. Too much opportunity to get a long piece of T.P. stuck to your shoe. O.K. freaky J, move on. Let's stay focused.

Hey, good news. The local hospital, where I'll be doing my blood work, doesn't have valet parking. Ahh, this is good. Would the booty spray work on the steering wheel? Stacey's SUV will surely be violated if we have to valet park. Dang, my stress o-meter is banging off the scales. O.K. freaky J, settle down.

Let me recap my sleep from last night. I usually sleep based on the need for rest and not a length of time. So, that probably explains why I roam the house at all hours. I always figure I can catch a nap later if needed. Remember, I'm the tumor-boy. Who would ever deny me a nap? It sounds good if someone calls on the phone, too. No Jeff can't come to the phone because he's in bed, napping. I think everyone expects me to be there anyway. So, there I lay.

Here is how I prepare for a nap or for bedtime. With this tumor, I know that there is always a possibility that I won't wake up. I think I now have the unique skill to forget to breathe. I believe the tumor could push on my brain and I could just stop breathing. This is always a comforting thought as my head hits the pillow. So, here is my routine when I prepare to get some shut-eye. Feet to the East and port side up. That would be my medi-port. You remember, my inverted shoulder nipple? Boy, I've had that thing accessed a time or two! O.K., back to my pre-sleep routine. I place a note on the nightstand. I put my name on the top: Jeff. #1-Breathe. So far, this is working well. Then I give the Lord thanks for the day he has given me and then I ask for a safe and restful sleep. I run over my prayer list that I keep in a notebook and then I pray for everyone that comes to mind. I eventually doze off. I find praying to be very comforting. So, falling asleep is pretty easy. I think when I fall asleep with a praying mind I seem to wake up in one. I immediately give Jesus thanks when I get up and give thanks that I can walk around. I give thanks when I can successfully negotiate around the widow makers. Maybe I should drop a pair of underwear on them to help me see them better, or at least smell them better. If Diane does a load of yellows today, I should have a few spare pair that I can leave at the top of the stairs as navigational markers. Boy, I'm always thinking! I think Diane believes that's my main problem. I have too much time to think. She's right.

What will she say about the fruity-booty spray idea? Well, she knows me all too well. So, she won't be surprised or impressed. I guess that's what twenty-five years of marriage will do to you. I know now why the Lord put me with her. I am blessed. If she had killed me when we first got married she would be on parole by now. That was a saying my dad would always use!

O.K., back to my day. Let's see, eat something or go back to bed? Maybe I'll just eat in bed or sleep on the kitchen counter? Hmm, too many decisions. I guess sleeping on the counter beats a dirt nap! Maybe.

In closing, I pray that you all have a blessed day and keep us in your prayers for healing and a full recovery. Please include Diane, the boys, the special chemo nurses at Hank, the tumor board, and Dr. Roy too. There is still a lot to do. May God bless you all! In the meantime, I'll be here working on my To-Do list.
Love- Jeff.

Chapter Thirty

Field Trip - Blood Draw

Apr 2 2009

Since I'm up early again, and probably missed last call somewhere, I'll recap my day yesterday. Anytime I get out of the house I feel like an elementary school kid going on a field trip. And, since my sister Stacey is a schoolteacher, it's appropriately named. The day out also gives Diane a much needed, although short, break. Caregivers need a break from time to time.

Stacey picked me up to take me to a nearby town to get my blood work done. After receiving a few last minute directions from Diane, we're off. The Old Jeff used to donate his blood to "give" the American Red Cross and had given nearly ten gallons over the years. But now, they "take" my blood. "Giving" blood sounds like a gentle procedure but "taking" it sounds like someone is holding you down, with a foot on your forehead, and aggressively removing it from your body. So yesterday, did I give blood or did they take it? I guess a little of both.

Nurse Jessica was new to me but she did a fine job. Before she started she asked me how I did giving blood? I said, huh? She clarified her question. "Do you pass out or have any problems during a blood draw?" I said, "Unless you're going to tap in the needle with your shoe, I should be o.k." I told her that I've given blood so many times that I look like a sprinkler when I take a drink of water. She laughed, and it eased her up a little bit. Next, she moves in for the kill and inserts the needle into my right arm. This arm resembles one that you might find on a drug addict, thanks to the track marks. After the needle is in I said, "Oh, you guys went back to using the square needles, huh?" She said, "Oh, I'm sorry, did that hurt?" It didn't so I said, "No, I was just kidding." She let out a nervous giggle, filled her glass tubes, and put on a band-aid and a $20 cotton ball.

Then, Stacey and I were on our way. The results will be faxed to the Hank and I'll be ready for my next round of chemo if the blood work looks good. It's kind of like waiting for Easter except Easter is more fun, unless you lose your bloody vial in the grass at the bottom of the basket. That's o.k. Maybe I'll find it next year, along with a dried up sugary peep, when I pull the basket from the attic? We'll see.

Stacey had some errands to do so we set out to get them done. Diane told her I needed a haircut so she guided me in that direction. Upon arriving at the quick-cuts salon, the girl looked at me and asked, "Do you have a punch-card for our brain surgery special?" "What's that" I asked. "Yeah", she continued. "We don't bang the clippers against the scar on your head and we trim those nasty eyebrows." "Hmm, that sounds like what I need" I said. "Let's do it. Can I get a new craniotomy coupon?" Is this chick blind? Whew! Did Diane call ahead as a cruel April fools day joke?

Anyway, this task is done so it's off to the mall. Once we got to the mall I can start to see her plan unfolding. In order to keep me from ping ponging into her as I walked next to her with my reduced peripheral vision, she decided to buy me a hot pretzel and set me down on a bench. When she ordered the pretzel, the girl asked what kind of dipping sauce I wanted. I said, "nacho cheese." But, it must have sounded like I said "nasty cheese" because that's what I got! Gross. Anyway, Stacey finds a bench and there I sit like a bump on a log. "Don't move, I'll be right back," she said. So I sit, but she never seems to come back. I'm now getting concerned that my PMS may flair up and throw me into a crying spell, which will surely get me a free trip to the mall's lost and found room. I wonder if they have chairs big enough to hold a full-grown man? Plus, just think how many kid-germs will be floating around in that room. Uh oh, don't panic.

I'm having thoughts that maybe Stacey is paying me back for locking her in the milk-house when she was four years old and leaving her there! Is she really paying me back all these years later? Oh man, hand me a tissue. Hey, here she is. She came back and I didn't even have to have my name called on the mall's loudspeaker. It was a good day, except I was short on money. So, she had to bail me out at the store. When she dropped me back at home, she told Diane that, on the next field trip, I'd need to bring an envelope with money and a permission slip. Boy, she does sound like a teacher. So, we'll have to comply. Diane will do anything to get me out of the house.

All in all, I was thankful for the day and grateful that I could walk through the mall. We talked about the times we took Mom and had to use a wheelchair. I used the mall as another opportunity to give God thanks! I'm thankful I didn't goose anyone during my mall walk. I don't know if anyone would buy my limited vision excuse? The mall cops would probably take my picture and post it somewhere calling me the groper!

In summary, we did a few more errands, including buying some college books for Brett, and then headed home. Thanks Stacey. A reminder to all…if you can get a care giver out of the house, even for a few minutes, try and take advantage of it. I'm sure the change of scenery and some fresh air will do them good. Have a blessed day and, as you can see, the note I left on my nightstand to remind me to breathe really worked well. The other day I was napping longer than usual. Diane tapped me on the shoulder and said, "I came to check on you to see if you were ok. You've been napping for a long time." I replied, "Did you think I was dead?" She laughed and said, "No, your color was good!" Hmm. I'm guessing that blue is a bad color?
Have a blessed day – Jeff

Chapter Thirty One

Smelly Feet

April 3, 2009

Since adjusting to life with cancer I've had a lot to deal with. And this next situation really stinks. Yesterday I walked into the living room and Diane is looking under the couch with a flashlight. I figured that whatever she lost was of great value. I said, "What are you looking for?" She said "food". I told her that maybe she should take her search to the kitchen. I don't think the last time I needed a loaf of bread or some soup that I went to the entertainment center in the living room. But, then again, I'm the guy shuffling around with my applesauce and yogurt, so maybe I misplaced it? I wouldn't put it past me. "O.K. Diane, I give up. What's going on?" "Well," she said. "Yesterday, when we were sitting on the couch, I smelled something real bad and now I am smelling it again!" I guess she could have left out the real bad part, especially since it was looking like I was somehow involved. Did she think this was how it was going to be now? In addition to dealing with me and my normal junk, she would now have to deal with me and some horrific odor? It sounds like I'll be carrying another tube or canister of something in my murse to combat my potential stink problem. I'd hate for the Hank valet team to open my car door and the funk smell be rushing out! They might end up giving me a nickname like Sir stinks-a-lot! Who knows?

O.K. Where was I? Diane is looking for food because she thinks that is the source of the bad odor she smelled. She was thinking that maybe Andrew or Brett dropped some type of food under the couch and that may be the cause of the odor she smelled. I've told those guys, "We don't sleep on the kitchen counters and we don't eat on the living room coffee table, so please make the necessary adjustments." Again, my advice fell on deaf ears. It's kind of like talking with my older brother Vic, except he has a valid excuse. He really does have deaf ears. Andrew and Brett just think Dada doesn't know much. If they only knew how right they are! They exposed me! I admit, I really don't know much and have been faking it for years.

Well, did my C.S.I. investigator wife find the "source o'stink?" I was hoping it wasn't a rogue pair of underwear. It wasn't. No, it turns out it was my feet. Dang, I need my feet. What will she ask the doctors to do, remove them? No, it wasn't actually my feet, but my slippers. Yep, these red and black fuzzy bacteria traps were the identified source of my new worry. Do they make a foot sanny and will it fit in my murse? I think I'm working my way up to the Nanny- Sanny, a full body spray. That should cover everything! Hmm, great idea. I should run with it, but not in these slippers! Man, what's a boy to do?

Anyway, through some good detective work and some intense interrogations, we located the culprit. Andrew. Oops, poor Andy goes under the bus, kind of. We found out that he has been wearing theses slippers on quick runs to the store or gas station. This attractive footwear and fashion statement would get damp if there was snow or rain in his path. Unknowingly, I would then wear them and my feet would warm them up, revealing the mysterious odor. Without the nanny sanny, there just isn't any way to cover up the funk. So, I took the fall on this one. But, at least we can close this case and I didn't have to take the full burden of the guilty sentence. Or worse, be placed under house arrest! I thought my fieldtrip days were over. I came out of this one smelling like a rose. I'm thinking a couple spins in the washing machine will fix these black and red bacteria traps. Also, I'll have to hide them. Maybe I can order one of those cardboard shoe holders that I see on T.V.? They slide right under the bed and I could guard these new fashion icons 24-7?

Right now I'm a little concerned that whenever something at the house is "just not right" everyone seems to look at me? I guess I'll have to pour on the PMS when I ask Andy to leave my slippers alone. He's getting used to my tears so maybe they won't work here. But, I guess if I slipped one of these black & red bombs under his pillow he'd get the message. That might be the answer, unless Diane has a better idea. We'll kick it around over breakfast. Remember, we have a few boxes of peanut butter crunch to polish off that was left over from the pity party. Man, that crunch stuff can sure tear up the inside of your mouth. It's like doing a crunchy-chemo thing without the hair loss. Hey, this peanut butter crunch stuff is making me thirsty!

Well, this was the unsolved mystery that was. Is there a lesson in here? Well, yes. As my Mom would always say, "The man with no shoes felt bad until he saw the man with no feet."

So, it's just another reminder that even if your feet stink, be thankful that you can still walk around. You know, I didn't even pre-plan that but I've been thanking the Lord for giving me the ability to do so much on my own. He has blessed me and blessed my family in so many ways that I cannot begin to understand how fortunate we are. He is taking good care of us and we thank Him constantly. – Amen.

Have a blessed day - Jeff

Chapter Thirty Two

E-mails

Posted Apr 4, 2009 4:54am

Since we seemed to avoid the latest computer virus I figured it would be a good time to clean up some old emails. So, I opened my email and here are some of the email subjects I found. I checked the subject titles in my inbox and one email subject told me that I could organize and protect my shoes with a "shoes under organizer." Hey, I saw this on TV. A cardboard box you store your shoes in under your bed. Would this novel invention withstand the odor of the black and red slippers? Could I store food in it just in case? Does it come with a light so Diane wouldn't have to look for a flashlight every time she suspects someone might be stashing food in the couch cushions? Does this cardboard organizer comes with a de-funk spray to mask any potential foot odors?

Another one read, "Recession proof jobs are in the nursing field." Wow, where to begin with this one? It sounds like good news to my friends at the Hank. They'll be the first ones to hook you up with a cotton ball that will cost about $20. If the wispy cotton ball is bacteria-free, I think the price is worth it. Do they ever drop one, kick it, and put it back in the package? Why did I even have to think about that? The thought of it could send me into sanitation frenzy. I'll have to ask the chemo nurses to ease my mind a little bit. I'll see them next week for my chemo treatment. I'll bring a cotton ball from home on that day just in case the answer to my question freaks me out. I'll be prepared.

Another email is telling me about getting a free insurance quote. I'm not sure if it's health or auto related insurance? I'm guessing, either way, one look at my Care Pages would probably disqualify me from any consideration for more insurance. They would see that this guy carries a murse full of creams and gels just to get through the next hour. Plus, throw in the blown tire from last week and I'm guessing the courtesy calls would stop rolling in.

Facebook. Oh man, who else wants to write on my wall? I need someone to paint my wall, not write on it. I get the same question. How are you doing? Hmm, where do I begin? I guess it would sound like this. Sometime after high school I had a bad headache that just wouldn't go away. Can I post that? Hey, let me put up a picture of my moon face. Do you recognize me? They would say, "Hmm, I don't think I want to be his friend. Who is he? Oh, it's bacteria-boy-09. I don't feel comfortable requesting him as my friend."

It's just freaky J blogging out loud. Is "Blogging Out Loud" a Hall and Oates album title? It should be. I think Oates is the little greasy guy. Not an A & D ointment greasy but let me look in my murse and see what I have to compare him to. Oh, preparation H. That might be it. Maybe on the album cover he could be holding one of my wax bullets between his fingers like a cigarette? Hmm, classy. Dang, that Jeff will type anything! Hate the play not the player! You have to be careful with those wax bullets. Whenever I feel the urge to sneeze I have to first do a quick inventory to see if I have one on-board. If I do, I'll have to readjust my next actions. I'm always planning ahead. The same holds true when you're packing a stool softener. I'll consider that a public service message. So, you've been warned.

Chapter Thirty Three

Jesus Statue

Posted Apr 7, 2009 5:36am

Giving thanks for what I can do April 3 2009 (rough week).

Since my cancer diagnosis I find myself comparing the Old Jeff to the New Jeff. The Old Jeff was a lot more independent and didn't have to rely upon others, unlike the New Jeff. If the Old Jeff needed water softener salt he just stopped at the hardware store after work and slung a few bags into the trunk and headed home. He truly knew the real meaning of having some junk in his trunk. Once home, he would haul it downstairs and pour it in the water softener. I know this example sounds pretty basic but now, when I have to rely on a whole supply chain to get this simple task done, I find myself getting discouraged.

Yesterday, I shifted my focus. I was truly thankful for everything I was doing for myself, and I mean everything. It didn't matter how trivial the task was. I would look at each part of the task and give thanks that I was doing it on my own. If part of the task was going into the basement, I was grateful that I could walk up and down the stairs on my own. I even avoided the dreaded Widow-makers that the boys strategically left at the top. You're probably thinking, 'Wow, Jeff's tumor must be growing fast. The dude already wrote on this subject and now he's doing it again. Well, I'm hopeful that the tumor is shrinking. And, I know I already wrote on this. But, I felt it was worth repeating, at least to myself. Most of my entries are helpful to me and I'm hopeful that, along the way, others may find them useful too.

I was thinking that I must have learned this grateful attitude from my mom, who had daily challenges dealing with her M.S. I could never understand how she was thankful for what she could do but, as I work through my own illness, I'm beginning to understand her life lessons. Thanks Mom!

O.K., going one step further, I am also thankful for the people in my life who act as my arms and legs. This brings me to a childhood story of the Jesus statue. When I was a young boy, I had a statue of Jesus that was on my dresser. He was plastic and stood about nine or ten inches tall. He just stood there but he held his arms out like he was carrying something. Eventually the statue lost his arms so He stood there holding out two stumps with no hands. As young kids and teenagers, Stacey and I would pass him back and forth anytime we would clean our rooms. So, every so often the missing Jesus statue would show up on my dresser, stumps and all. Or, on the rare occasion I would clean my room I would load a box of knick-knacks, put Jesus in the box, and send it to her room. We did this back-and-forth thing because we couldn't bring ourselves to throwing Jesus away. One day, while I was in college, I picked up a box from my dad's house and took it to Detroit, where I was living. As I was unloading the box, there was the Jesus statue with the loose arms. I knew it was a gift from Stacey, and I was right.

So, what's my point? I think my point is this. Like the Jesus statue, He was showing us that we need to be his arms, hands and legs. Hmm. Heavy! Even though there are things that I can't do for myself there are others in my life that can. And, they are more than willing to do so. Unlike the Hall and Oates song that says "No Can Do." Jesus says, "Do!" By the way, which one was Hall and which one was Oates? I could never keep those two guys straight.

This afternoon, Brett went grocery shopping for Diane and I. I explained this story to him and told him thanks for being our arms and legs. He understood. Maybe the message was for him. I'll share this story with Andrew tomorrow. He's always willing to be our arms and legs, too. So is Victor, Ann-Marie, Ken, Mike, Duane, Scott, Tom, Jim D., Jim S., Cameron, John, Jibber, Nathan, Stacey, and the list goes on. The strongest arms I have are Diane's. She somehow keeps it all together.

OK, 'nuff preachin' Mister. Yeah, I hear ya! I'm learning that sometimes just shifting my focus from the "can't" to the "can" is enough to get me over the rough parts of my day. And, since I'm in survival mode, I'll use whatever I can. It's sort of like opening a fresh tube of the infamous A & D ointment! Oh man, may my day be blessed and my murse never be empty!

Chapter Thirty Four

MRI

Posted Apr 8, 2009 8:22pm

Today was my MRI day and it started off as a typical day. This means Diane yelled at me because I wasn't ready to roll at the appointed time. I told her I would be telling Stacey that she yelled at me but it didn't seem to faze her. I think Stacey would be on her side anyway. It was my fault so I'm sure I had it coming. I didn't have my routine of turning off yard lights and stuff like that done and we needed to get going to make it to the Hank on time. Usually we have traffic and snow to deal with but today was light traffic and no snow. Ann-Marie met us at the MRI area and it was nice to see her. Sounds like a good start.

After the MRI, we met with Dr. Roy to review the results. The MRI showed signs that the tumor was progressing. There was some slight growth with two new small spots. Here is my take on it; clinically, I'm still doing as well as I was six months ago. Also, there is another clinical trial that I may be able to participate in. The Tumor Board will discuss it and let me know in a day or two. Without the new tumor growth maybe the trial wouldn't be open to me and maybe this trial will be a good match for my body. I don't know. It's always possible that the MRI could have been much worse. Again, I don't know the Lord's plan but I'm still hopeful for His healing.

Dr. Roy was a little nervous leaving me in the exam room by myself. He thought I might try scratching my tumor through my nose and wipe it on the edge of his desk. He should be pleased that I didn't have an itch today. Anyway, I left the room in tact. He did check to make sure I had my wallet though. You see, he's from the Philippines and I think he has a rickshaw payment coming due. Learning that he received some of his training in the Philippines, I did have to ask him if he trained on real patients or on coconuts? Hmm. I was surprised when he said "coconuts" but there probably isn't a whole lot of difference between a coconut and my noggin. Hey, whatever works I guess? We also ran into Tammy in the hallway and she had a dirty cotton ball for me. She'll probably be charging us extra for the added labor cost of getting it dirty. She always brightens up our day when we see her and today was no exception. The crazy redhead! Oh, a good kind of crazy!

Since I need to do a washout of the old chemo from my system before I can take the new trial meds, I didn't have treatment today. Bottom line is this may be good news. Again, we'll know someday.

I updated Brett, Andrew, Stacey, Victor, and some others on the way home from the Hank. I am thankful for having a good support team that takes care of me! Thanks for the prayers. Love, Jeff & Diane. So, I'm counting today as a good day.

Chapter Thirty Five

My Siblings

Posted Apr 11, 2009 7:54am

Lately, when I think I'm having a bad day, I find myself picking up the phone and calling my brother and sisters just to hear their voices. I'm thankful that most days are good, but every once in a while just hearing their voices is comforting. Plus, this gives Diane, Brett, and Andrew a break from having to watch ol' Dad cry again! "What's Dad's deal anyway?" Andrew says I need to wear a manpon. Hmm, I hear what he's saying and I think he's right. I don't think I'm hiding my PMS too well! Wait! Let me check my murse to see if I have room to carry a couple manpons. The murse is getting full. The other day I spoke with Nancy, my insurance agent, and she told me to put my roadside assistance stuff for the car in my murse. I told her "I couldn't live like that," which is my dad's famous quote.

Getting back to my siblings. I had a great childhood, thanks to them. Stacey was like my little brother. "Hey Stacey, put on this catcher's gear and let me throw some fastballs at you" I'd yell. "Come on, toughen up!" She was a good sport. Ann-Marie was my social network over-seer. She made sure my clothes matched for school and that I had a decent haircut. One time she was using a library book and flipping the pages as she was cutting my hair. I remember getting half way through the cut, flipping the page, and hearing her say, "Uh, Oh!" If you look at my 5th grade school photo you'll see the lump of hair on the top of my head that never caught on in the fashion world. We grew closer as we made our way into high school.

Victor and I were Dad's right-hand men. He always had some type of project for us to work on. We usually ended up in a fistfight but we got the job done. It wasn't until Victor left for college that I finally realized how important he was to me. I learned a lot from him just by watching him. Since what he said never made any sense, maybe the watching thing was a good idea? He was, and is, a great people-person and treats everyone so well. He has a good work ethic and is always willing to jump in and help, even when it doesn't benefit him. He was, and is still, a great brother.

To this day, Ann, Stacey, and Vic are a huge support system for Diane and me. We are thankful for them daily and know that they are only a phone call away. I'm writing this because I just want to remind them that I'm proud to call them sister and brother.

I have another letter to write which will go to Andrew and Brett, and I'm not ready to write it yet. I'll need more tissues. So, I'll just work on the siblings' letter for now. Thanks for all of your support Ann-Marie, Stacey, and Vic. I know Diane can rely on each of you if needed. I love you guys! Since Mom and Dad have both passed away I can look to my brother and sisters for any life lesson that they left for me.

Again, I am truly blessed!

Chapter Thirty Six

Sounds Like A Memory

April 12 2009

Yesterday, the weather here in Michigan was very mild. I was able to spend a little time outside enjoying the sunshine and was grateful for it. One thing I noticed is the sounds that would remind me of different times in my life. As I mentioned earlier, I sometimes call my brother or sisters just to hear their voices. I think this is all part of the same thing. Just as certain songs may trigger a memory, so will other sounds. The first thing I heard was the siren from an ambulance, which is kind of rare to hear out here in the country. I heard it coming in the distance and was wondering if it was coming for me? I quickly ran into the house to see if Diane found the underwear I had hidden and had made a proactive call to 911 (because she would surely kill me if she found them). Well, all was good, and no call was placed. Whew! But it got my attention.

The siren reminded me that perhaps someday that siren sound would be coming for me. It got me thinking. If it does come for me, when? Hmm, I don't know. On that day, would they take me out of the house through the garage entrance or the front door? I know, they're freaky questions, but living with this illness brings on some weird thoughts and sometimes it only takes a small trigger to start thinking about it. If I go out the garage, will the ambulance guys scrape the cars? Will they drop the gurney with me still strapped onto it? Other than the dropping thing I guess I shouldn't worry too much about the car scraping. Maybe I'll keep some foam strips ready just in case. You know me, always trying to plan ahead. Do I need to put a hook on my murse so I can hang it on the stretcher? Man, I can't forget that little bag of goodies. I should drop a hand mirror in there too. Just in case I need to check my look.

Back to the ambulance, the siren sound soon faded out of earshot. I wondered where it was going and with whom? It reminded me of my prayer list so prayers went out with that ambulance.

I also heard a song that day that reminded me of my mom. It's called "Bubbly." That was the first thought trigger I heard for the day, which then reminded me of my dad. It was a two-for-one special. I sure do miss them both. I then heard a car coming. It sounded like Brett's Mustang but, unfortunately, it wasn't. Later in the day I told him I wish I still had my Mustang. "We could park them side-by-side and vacuum them out" I told him. He looked at me and I'm sure he was thinking, "Yeah, we could park them side-by-side and you could vacuum them both," he replied. And, of course, I would. I loved cleaning up my cars and I'm sure I'll clean a few more before I take the old dirt nap or go for my ride with the nice man in the van with the flashing lights. I'm planning on it. I just hope I don't have to take a ride with the men in the nice white suits. You know, the guys that work at the Hotel – Crazy!! I'm sure they have a nice padded room for me. Hey, maybe I can get my foam there?

Andrew was playing his guitar before dinner, which reminded me of when his band would practice in our basement. Wow. They were loud and it got intense at times but it would sure be nice to have them back. I bet I wouldn't complain as much. Sometimes Diane and I couldn't even hear each other talk because they were so loud. But, I bet they wouldn't seem so loud if we had to do it all over again.

What do I hear now? A motorcycle? Yep. It reminds me of my last trip which I took just days before my diagnosis. That would have been in the July 2007 time frame. I guess I probably didn't need to wear my helmet on that trip. But, of course I did. You know, I wouldn't want to injure my tumor! Anyway, what about the bike trip you ask? Well, I'll tell you about it. My buddy, Uve from Norway set up a trip with a motorcycle travel company to travel Route 66 from Hollywood. I told him I would meet him in the Chicago area on my motorcycle (a.k.a. bike). I was going to ride with my cousin John but, due to some last minute changes in schedule, I made the trip alone. The plan was to ride through the Upper Peninsula of Michigan and then into Milwaukee and then into The Windy City to meet my Norwegian buddy. Who, by the way, says you can always tell a Norwegian but you can't tell them much. Oh, that was my cousin's comment. Pretty accurate I think! I scheduled the trip to take about a week to complete.

Day one: It was raining hard but I pushed forward so I could meet my schedule. I packed my clothes in big; body condom sized bags and loaded my bike. I put on my rain gear and said my good-byes to Diane and headed west on I-69. It was raining pretty hard but I didn't let that interrupt my trip. I've done the rain thing many times and didn't worry about it this time either. As long as I stay dry I can ride. I stopped near Saginaw, Michigan to take a break, call home and get a hot cup of coffee. So far, so good. It was nice to hear Diane's voice on the other end of the phone. I rested for an hour, suited back up and hit I-75 northbound. The bike is running fine and I'm relatively dry even after riding in the rain for a few hours. I needed the body condom but, since it wasn't invented yet, I relied on my motorcycle rain gear and it seemed to be doing the trick. My goal was to get to Sault Saint Marie, Michigan by 5PM that evening and get checked into a hotel.

I made my goal and, after grabbing a quick dinner at a local greasy spoon restaurant, I unloaded my bike and tried to settle into my room for the night. I remember having a headache but I figured it was due to the cold, damp weather I had been riding in for the last few hours. Hmm… if I had only known? This made me edgy. I asked for a room away from the hotel's service door because every time someone came in it would slam and wake me up. But, the two young girls at the front desk couldn't seem to help me out. "Sorry" just didn't seem to help. I usually don't run into too much confrontation with people but these girls bordered on being useless. I now realize that some of the problem was me. The tumor was swelling and pushing on my brain so I was easily agitated, just ask Diane! Ha Ha. I noticed that the sliding window in my hotel room did not have a security latch so I was thinking of breaking the legs off of the little table in the room and using one of the table legs to wedge into the window frame. But, I didn't. I just let it go. Again, this was another tumor issue since I usually don't break up hotel room furniture. I'll leave that for the rock stars. Oh, the cable TV was out too. My two helpful friends said the entire state of Michigan was out because someone cut the cable. Yeah sure, I thought. If this nice hotel stay doesn't improve maybe I will tear up some furniture! Another biker gone bad!

I eventually slept that first evening. I got up early the next morning, grabbed some breakfast and headed north out of Marquette, Michigan on I-75. No rain and it looked like it was going to be a sunny day.

I crossed the Mackinaw Bridge, which put me up into Michigan's Upper Peninsula. I then headed west toward Green Bay, Wisconsin. But, the weather report would drastically change my schedule. Since I was riding alone I could make any changes I needed as long as I agreed with myself. Lately, this was becoming an issue. It's good I didn't agree to tear up the hotel before I rolled out of town. Wisconsin declared a state of emergency because of floods. The news reports said they closed the jails so they could relocate the inmates to an area that wasn't flooded. After I got a good weather update, I decided to abort my trip and headed for home. At this point I was about a four-hour ride from home. I rode across the U.P. and then headed south. My plan was to get home and take my car to Chicago. Still dealing with headaches, I was glad when I pulled into my garage at home. A hug from Diane was great medicine. I can feel it now.

Later that same day my headache and me headed out to Chicago, which is about a six-hour car ride. I remember it was a tiring ride, even in a car, because I was not feeling well. But, I eventually made it to Chicago and met Uve for dinner at a local hotel. The hotel was directly across the street from an area landfill and I can still remember the stench. It was the most awful smell I can remember. The smell was from the water they use to run over the trash to rinse it. I remember waking up in the morning. Headache? Yes. Sinus problem? Probably. Landfill stench? Yes, but not as bad as the black and red slippers.

The next day I couldn't wait to leave Illinois and get home. So I rolled out and made it home. It was a long trip but a good ride, all in all. The toughest part was traveling with the headaches. My bike had so much grime on it from the rain that it would eventually take a lot of extra cleaning, but I got 'er done. I also noticed that the stinky landfill smell was still inside my car. The interior absorbed the odor. It was nasty. I can still smell it in my mind. Wow, that was some nasty funk! Even a week later the funk would rush out when I opened my car door. Okay, great trip, but a stinky trip. I'm grateful to have ridden it safely considering the tumor I was hauling along with me. A few weeks later, I would receive the fateful news that I had cancer. Who would have guessed it?

Thank you, Lord for allowing me to take this trip and return home safely. I was blessed again but didn't know it at the time. I think if I had to sum it up, I would say that on this trip there were several opportunities that could have changed me from how I am today. So, I am again thankful for everything that I can do for myself and grateful that I will have closure with all of my loved ones. I am reminded again that I am truly blessed. - Jeff

Chapter Thirty Seven

I'm a Mess

As my mother was going through life with multiple sclerosis, this was a phrase that she would often repeat to get us laughing. My siblings and I have heard it so often that we just say the words to each other now for a good laugh. Mom would never complain about anything. I think I'll try and sum up where she was emotionally and physically when she said this phrase. I have adopted this phrase into my own vocabulary because "I AM a mess." If I catch Diane laughing at something I've done that seems a little strange I'll just throw the words out there. It's a great stress reducer believe it or not. If I try and put my slippers in the drawer or the milk jug in the cupboard I just say "oops!" Then, after a long pause, I'll say "I'm a mess" and I'm quickly out of trouble. It works every time.

I think what was happening was Mom would compare herself to others or to her old self. For example, if she would knock over her water glass and get her books wet someone would grab a towel and try to initiate some damage control. As she looked at the wet books and table she'd say, "I'm a mess." We'd giggle and move on or, as we were wiping up the water, we'd say, "You're a mess." And the laughter would start. It was a good way to easily diffuse any situation. I never tried this tactic at work and I often wonder if it would work there? Would it work if I was stopped for speeding or if I accidentally slammed a shopping cart into a car at the grocery store? It probably wouldn't get you out of immediate trouble but I guess I could try it one day. I guess if the I.R.S. would buy it anyone would. But, I don't think I'll try that one. I would probably be the only one laughing! And I WOULD be a mess.

What if I got onto the elevator at the Hank and pressed the wrong button? After everyone inside the bacteria box settled down could I just say, "Oops, I'm a mess" and press another button? Well, I see two problems here. One is that I would have to touch two buttons. Yuk! Secondly, I would have to spend an additional sixteen seconds inside the box o' funk. Quick, get me out of here. I'm the blue guy in the back who's holding his breath. Clear a path! Did I leave my murse in there? Where's my Hanny–Sanny?

Well, I think I just came up with something funkier than an elevator button or a railing on a set of stairs. What about that key that is attached to a stick at a roadside gas station's restroom? Can you imagine the crud on that thing? O.K., you've all been warned! We need to make up some posters. What do they call that invention, a crap stick? When you ask for the restroom key and the clerk goes to hand it to you, don't accept it. Just say, "I'm a mess" and then stand there and wet yourself. It sounds like your safest option, unless you have a big ol' can of fanny-sanny! Would a condom fit onto the restroom key stick? Hmm. Sounds like a good investment. Make sure you always carry an extra quarter. I'm feeling the urge to wash my hands. Did I ever put the fecal stick (a.k.a., crap stick) under my chin after I unlocked the door? Oh, surely not! Wow, I am a mess, but who's laughing? I need to move off this stick thing, and quickly, before I ruin my whole week. Maybe Diane's Aunt Diane from Texas can send me a new mini bottle of hand sanitizer, and quickly! If the Hank valet guy ever hands me my car keys attached to a stick I'll walk home! And, I won't be tipping him. He probably already found my eleven cents in the glove box anyway. Oh no, here we go again. Man, I really am a mess.

Knowing that we're a mess keeps us sane and we can begin to make some changes. I think it's called self-awareness. On some level we're really all a mess. I think Mom was on to something. We just need to make sure we don't focus on it too intently but realize that we are who we are. That is how the Lord wants us to be. It's all part of the big picture and we can't, or shouldn't, focus on our differences or shortcomings. Be joyful with what we have and who we are. I know it's easier said than done. But, keep relying on God.

Chapter Thirty Eight

A Different Perspective

Yesterday I started a new chemotherapy treatment and am hopeful, and prayerful, that it will work. After Diane and I arrived at the Hank, a nickname I gave my hospital, I settled into my comfortable green vinyl recliner and said "I hate coming here." After realizing what I had just said I quickly added, "Well, it beats NOT coming here!" I then realized that I am thankful for the life sustaining drugs they are giving me and I'm hopeful that the latest combination of drugs will hold this tumor at bay.

Yesterday, Diane and I made it through the chilly day, the treatment, and the long drive to and from the hospital. We even stopped at the funeral home to visit a young family friend who recently passed away from a tumor similar to mine. We didn't stay at the funeral home for long because the funeral director kept following me around with a tape measure. What was his deal? He must have seen me as some economic stimulus!! I told Diane about him and her advice was this, "Whatever you do, don't stop moving and don't go in that other room over there!" Hmm, sounds like some simple advice that I can follow.

This morning I woke up and noticed on the counter top some of the paperwork and meds that we brought home from the Hank. I was trying to stay positive but these visual reminders were bringing me down. I saw a copy of my MRI scan, my calendar of doctor's visits, and the new chemo drug bottle complete with a long list of side affects I can expect while taking it. I guess loss of appetite is not one of them because I was hungry. But, I couldn't find any bread in the cupboard. I did find some kind of cinnamon swirl bread that I could toast up, so I did. I remembered Diane had bought some cinnamon cream cheese and the mini meal was taking shape, or so I thought. Did you know, under certain lighting conditions, tuna fish looks a lot like cinnamon cream cheese? I guess one of my sons was saving the leftover tuna for lunch, unless he thought ol' dad wanted it for breakfast? Mmm, delicious! Fish and coffee!

I was still in my funky mood after seeing all of the visual reminders of my cancer so I thought I would check my email. I opened an email that was titled "prayer request." These normally get top priority when I check my email. So, if I owe you money and you need to remind me, just put prayer request in the e-mail's subject line and I'll get right to it. It could read something like this. Jeff, I pray you send me the money you owe me! This particular prayer request was from the motorcycle ministry I belong to and it was a request from a seventeen-year-old kid who was in jail. His plea for prayer was pretty heavy duty. He sounded desperate. Desperate that God would intervene and comfort him. Suddenly, my tuna fish toast didn't look (or smell) so bad. I placed him on my prayer list and prayed for him. I knew that the Lord was trying to get my attention this morning. This young man's name was Jeff, although he spelled it in the old school way (Geoff). But, I got the message. His jail was brick and mortar. My jail was in my own mind. I guess this prayer request was my own get out of jail card. I'll cancel my pity party. I really doubt anyone was going to come to it anyway once they heard tuna and cinnamon toast was on the menu. Hey, party on!

In summary, this was another lesson from my Lord that I need to rely on Him. Like I said before, I'm not sure how anyone can go through a bad situation or a life-threatening illness without having an open dialog with God. Amen. I am truly blessed. – Jeff.

Chapter Thirty Nine

Time

April 15, 2009

Yesterday was my first day after the new chemo and I think everything went well. Diane and her friend Cheryl went grocery shopping so I just hung out at our house. The chemo will lower my resistance to fight infections so they recommend avoiding sick people. I'm not sure why they have me go to the Hank every week? That place is loaded with sick people! Hmm. Maybe I'll ask them what's up with that?

I have my green masks ready just in case a visitor stops by the house. Cheryl brought her own mask and I used a green one when Jim W. came over. Cheryl's mask was white, so I hope it was U.S.D.A. approved. I think I'll be O.K. Appetite was good yesterday. Fatigue was not too bad either. What did I do yesterday? I took a couple naps. Did dishes. Dang, with all of the activity around here, I guess I won't ever have to worry about running out of green masks! In the afternoon I sat in the living room just thinking. Yes, I did record it on the calendar. April 14th…Jeff…Thinking. Maybe I wrote Jeff…thunk? I'll check. As I sat there the clock on the wall was going tic toc. Maybe it was more of a click, click, click. I don't think it made a toc sound but hey, it's my blog! Anyway, the sound of time ticking away was a solemn reminder of life. As the seconds ticked away I wondered whether this symbolized another second closer to death or another second further from birth? I guess it depends on what's in your murse!! I don't think either scenario matters. We know that you can't store up time or save it for later. We need to use the time we have. You can't buy more time either! They say you can't give it away but maybe that's the best use of it. Give your time to others. Bless them. Maybe that's the key?

As I sat, I had a few time regrets. But, I realized I made the best use of the time I was given, or so I thought at the time I used it. I can't go back and change anything so I think this was a good conclusion.

OK - moral of this blog. You can't change the past so don't freak out if you see parts of your life where you may have wasted time! Just focus on the time at hand and do the best you can with it. Have a great day and I'll be in touch if the good Lord is willing and the creeks don't rise!! May God bless you all and I would like to thank everyone who gave us their time! - Jeff

Chapter Forty

Brothers - Teaching

Posted Apr 16, 2009 4:54am

I woke up early again today with a slight headache. It must be that darn sinus issue I've been dealing with. I looked in the mirror and saw the axe handle sticking out of my head so maybe it's not a sinus problem? Brett and Andrew went to a music concert last night so they should be rolling in shortly. When they do something together they call it "Broday", which is short for Brother's day. I'm glad they're spending time together. Even though they have the same parents and were raised under the same roof they're as different as night and day. Which, I guess, is pretty common for siblings.

I was looking at some old photos yesterday and remembered how they learned to ride bikes many years ago, no thanks to Dad. I'm not a good bike teacher. Andrew was about four years old when he learned. Brett, on the other hand, started to worry me. I was afraid he would be the only grandfather that didn't know how to ride a two-wheeler. One summer day Diane, the boys and I were at her grandfather's and all the kids were riding their bikes. Andrew came in the house and asked if I could get his bike out of the trunk so he could ride. I said "Sure, no problem." As I was pulling his bike out I saw that one training wheel was broken. I handed him his bike and said, "You won't be able to ride this it's broken." He said, "Can you take off the other training wheel?" I replied, "Sure, but you can't ride this bike like this." Hmm, I ended up eating those words. About an hour later he calls me outside to show me he can ride his bicycle. To this day I can still hear myself telling him "You won't be able to ride this bike, it's broke." Boy, was I wrong. I'm glad my words of discouragement didn't stop him, even at the ripe old age of four. I was really proud of him when he showed me I was wrong and that he could learn in spite of what I told him. I was a proud poppa!

Brett was getting older and still not riding on two wheels. I was getting nervous. What if someone saw him? What was my plan to teach him? I call it the "Dad must be insane" plan, which is not sold in bookstores near you. Thank God. Sorry, Brett. Here is what I did. Let me run through my checklist. Bike? Check. Helmet? Check. Hill? Check. Pads? Check. One worried son? Check that! O.K., it sounds like we're ready. The plan was simple. Put boy on bike. Take bike and boy to top of hill. Push boy and bike down the hill. Wow, what in the world was I thinking? I think I know why? Desperation! Maybe my tumor was in its infant stage?? Did our driver's training lessons sound like this? "O.k., when I drop this brick on the accelerator just steer down this ramp and hold on. Be careful! Oh, buckle up! I'll meet you at the hospital." Thankfully I didn't teach him to drive a car using that method.

After a few crashes and a lot of tears he figured it was safer to learn on his own rather than have the two most trusted hands in his life push him to his death. So, he eventually learned to ride his bike. Today, he can even ride a motorcycle. Brett, I'm sorry. If I ever end up in a wheel chair please let Andrew push me. We're good, me and you, O.K.? Aren't we??

I think I learned that everything works out in due time, and it did. I was thinking that there was a set age limit when kids should be riding a bike but I was wrong. In God's timing everything is perfect, even if it looks hopeless at the moment. I bet Brett wishes I knew this back then.

Brett reminded me of when I taught him to write his name in kindergarten, he thought I was going to cut his fingers off! OK, that sounds like a tumor thing!! He's probably glad he learned to shave on his own! Yeah, I'm sure of that one. So, trust in God's timing. And never, ever, ever, ever, ever use the bunny hill to teach your kids to ride a bike. I don't know too many people over twenty who can't ride a bicycle so they'll eventually learn. I'm sure this lesson applies to everything in life from long division to kicking a football. So, be a source of encouragement not a hindrance. Everything in due time! And yes, this clearly shows that I'm a nut case.

Chapter Forty One

What We See

Posted Apr 19, 2009 7:24pm

Yesterday I was reminded that what we get is often exactly what we asked for, although it sometimes looks different. Kind of like trail mix. We can ask for trail mix but each bag looks different. But, it's still trail mix. Does that make sense? I got answers to some of my prayers but the answers looked different than I was expecting. But, when I really thought about it, they were definitely the right answers.

A good example is the flat tire we had on treatment day a few weeks back. I asked for safe travels to and from the Hank that day and it's possible that the delay we had that morning prevented us from a car accident later that morning. Things often look different than they are, even though it's what we asked for or what we need. I hope that makes sense? I reread that line and I think I may have laid on the axe handle a little too long? Hmm. I'd better stop into the lumberjack camp for a quick adjustment, although I'm feeling pretty well this morning.

Another example? OK. Back in my riding days I asked for a murse, which I now have, but I didn't expect to be hauling it around full of baby wipes, waxed bullets, ointments, rubber underwear, and salves. But, I did ask for the bag. So you see, what we ask and pray for is usually what we get. But, it's sometimes hard to recognize because it comes in a different form. It looks different than what we were expecting, kind of like the old 'don't judge a book by its cover' story.

This reminds me of my buddy, Hollis. I first saw Hollis at our church several years ago while he was serving food to the guests after a wedding service. My exposure to "church people" was probably typical to most of you...suit, tie, etcetera. But, the day I met Hollis, I thought the only suit he ever owned was probably issued from the county jail. Sorry bro! It must be the tumor talking again! This tumor seems to get me out of a lot of trouble! Over time I got to know him and saw that he was truly a man of God, long hair and all. His exterior has nothing to do with what's inside. But, I know we often look at the exterior and make our judgments. When we do this we overlook a lot of good books and a lot of good people. And yes, I'm a slow learner but I'm trying. Remember, it took me eating four pounds of trail mix before it dawned on me that this much roughage might not be good for me. I guess Nurse Bob with the big fingers was an answer to a prayer, although I didn't ask for the big fingers! I wonder how he's been doing? Ah man, where am I going with this? Quick, back to story.

Looking back over the past few days I have seen some answers to prayers but the answers were not what I had expected. But, I can see that they were answered and I am thankful. I know the Lord has a better plan for me than the one I have for myself. He is in control so any answer to prayer is an answer indeed. Long story short, don't judge a book by its cover. Or, it is not necessary to pick around the funky nuts in life's bag of trail mix because you may miss some good ones.

Chapter Forty Two

The Anchor

Posted Apr 21, 2009 8:28pm

Some days there always seems to be an overriding theme in my life that ends up being my topic of the day. Today it is an anchor. I read in my daily devotional this morning that Jesus is our anchor and, in order to see how strong the anchor is, we need to go through some storms. I know we all have storms in our lives. A family friend, Mrs. B., is in the high seas in a storm right now. So, please keep her and her family in your prayers. Thanks!

When the anchor is thrown you'll know how strong it is. Throw it and trust. Today, I had to keep reminding myself of those words and found it very helpful. My stress level has been a little high these past days and I'm learning that stress will wear you out! I thought a colon full of trail mix was stressful, but regular ole stress seems to be a little worse. Hey, don't get me wrong. I'm not advising you to knock down a four-pound bag of the "Mix". But, I think it's important to keep your worries and stress down and out of your life. So keep focused that Jesus is your anchor. I can tell you that it really does help. You'll feel a lot better… inside and out.

This evening I didn't have much of an appetite so Diane made me some oatmeal. When I got to the snack bar I see a bowl of oatmeal, a glass of juice, a piece of toast, and 13 almonds on a napkin. Oh man, I'm really stressed now. What do I do with the almonds? Do I eat them on the way to the emergency room or will I be OK? I don't even know if Nurse Bob is working or on-call tonight.

Earlier today my brother Vic and sister Stacey took me to the hospital, where Bob works, for blood work. We got in and out without incident or even a football style tap on the butt from Bob. So, it was a good trip. I didn't even see him! I did get a free lunch out of the deal too. I played the "I don't have any money" card when the bill came. Works every time. Stacey told me that card is worn out. Not to worry. I'll be sure Diane corrects that situation or they won't take me on any more field trips. I enjoyed the day and time with Vic and Stacey. Yes, you guessed it. My PMS was working overtime. I cried a lot but we did have a good day together. I am truly blessed with my brother and sisters.

Be blessed and throw your anchor when the stress is getting the best of you. It does help, so try it. Prayers for Mrs. B and family.

God bless you all. - Jeff

Chapter Forty Three

Doctor Visit

April 23, 2009

Stacey took me to the Hank yesterday for my normal doctor's visit. It was a routine visit where they check my vitals and see how I'm doing clinically. We left early and had good weather and traffic. So, it was a good morning all around. Yes, Diane did send me with money, so I'm sure that made Stacey happy. I forgot my permission slip but Miss Stacey let me on the bus anyway. I didn't cause her any problems by asking her to turn around and take me back home either. So, it was a good trip. Diane gave me a good talking to before I left home and I didn't want Miss Stacey telling on me and getting me in trouble. I behaved and pretty much followed the rules. I'm a slow learner but at least I'm learning.

The Doctor's check up was good. He checked my blood counts and then looked me over and checked my vitals. They were all fine. I'll have another MRI around the end of May and that will let us know how the chemotherapy is doing. We stopped for a quick lunch and I ordered a kid's happy meal since I wasn't too hungry. The toy that came with it was a big plastic finger and his name was Bob. True story. It was kind of creepy. I think it's a character from a movie that's going to be released soon. It was creepy, especially since the finger's name was Bob! Kind of freaky the more I think of it. I think Bob is headed for the garbage. I know I definitely won't be putting it in my murse!

Stacey and I had a nice visit and I enjoyed spending some time with her. Plus, Diane was able to get a break from me. But then again, that's my opinion. She may certainly disagree. Thank you all for your on-going prayers and have a blessed weekend. You're all in my prayers. God bless you all. Jeff

Chapter Forty Four

Our Family Trip
April 24, 2009

In our living room there is a photo of a younger Jeff and Diane and two small boys. Those boys are Brett and Andrew. My brother Vic, took the picture in 1998 in Northern California. I would have to say it's one of my favorite pictures. It brings back lots of memories. Lately, when I look at it, I wonder if the tumor was in its early stages. I guess it really doesn't matter since I can't change the past and I can't do anything about it now. What I can do is cherish the memories from the trip, both the good and the bad. What could have been bad? Well, when you get me involved anything can happen.

I had a lot of frequent flyer miles and some free hotel stay coupons from the company I was working for at the time so the cost of the trip was very inexpensive. We stayed at Vic's place in San Francisco for a few days too. Since this was our first big family trip I figured I would get the most out of the trip. So, in order to do this, I would have to optimize every minute. This is where it went wrong. Here is what my schedule looked like. 8AM breakfast. 8:04 AM load up and head to next destination, etc. I had so much crammed into the schedule that we probably missed a lot of stuff along the way, not to mention the stress that my schedule caused.

We drove the Pacific Coast Highway to Los Angeles, went to Alcatraz Island, visited the Golden Gate bridge, and the list goes on. We did, and saw, just about everything you could imagine in California. But, with my crazy schedule, I bet we missed a lot along the way. The family time was nice but nut-bag Jeff was a little over the top as the event coordinator. We never slowed down to smell the roses, but we have learned a lot from that trip. All future trips have been a lot more enjoyable and more loosely structured so we could enjoy the trip and take in the sights and sounds. I often wonder if this is how we go through life, rushing around and missing out on the joy and the company of our friends and family? I would have to say, "yes" since we always try to keep to our schedule. Maybe our schedules are too busy?

Long story short, enjoy those around you and be grateful that they're part of your life at this very moment. I think this is a good lesson for all of us. I'm a slow learner so the reflection back on our trip was a blessing for me. I'm grateful that Diane, Andrew, Brett and Vic were my teachers of this very important lesson of the day. Thanks y'all!! I enjoyed the time with you. Love Dad. Love Jeff.

Andrew and Jeff – 1988

Jeff and Miss Stacey before
one of their road trips

Diane's Dad, Butch and Jeff - Now they love each other

Jeff and his niece "Kelsey-Chelsey"

Jeff, Diane and his niece "Cayla-Bea"

Diane's Family, Donnie, Donna, Butch, Linda, Darla and Diane

Jeff with his cousin Scott 2008

Norm (Jeff's Dad), Jeff and Andrew - 1989

Jeff and nephews, Cameron and Patrick - July 2008

Jeff and Diane – 1982

Jeff and Diane – 2001

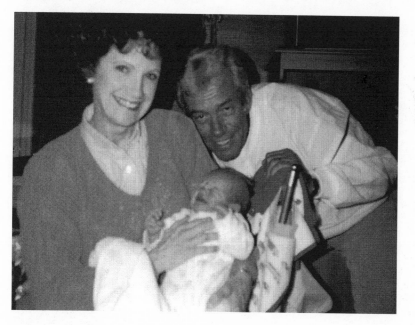

Brett with Jeff's Mom and Dad - 1989

Jeff, Andrew and Brett – 1990

Jeff's Dad, Norm - 2003

Jeff and Dr. Roy – 2009

Photo taken in 2005 when Jeff got his Harley

Jeff and twin nephews, Adam and Brian - 2008

Brother in-law Mike and Uncle Roger

Ann-Marie, Jeff and Stacey

Freakin- Family Fun Night - Jeff, Ann, Vic & Stacey

The Men - Jeff and son's Brett and Andrew

Jeff and Diane's Mom, Linda

Diane and Jeff – 2009

Diane, Jeff and youngest son Brett

Jeff and Diane - Senior Prom 1982

Diane and Jeff's wedding – November 1984

Captain Jeff

Our Family – One of Jeff's favorite photos taken on their trip to California

Jeff and Stacey – Stacey was really Robin (couldn't find a Robin sweatshirt)

Jeff and Diane 2006 - There's the classic Jeff look

Jeff and his oldest son Andrew 2006

Jeff and Diane renewing their wedding vows in Vegas – Elvis officiating

At youngest son Brett's graduation from High School in 2008

Jeff and his mom just after his first brain surgery – September 2007

Feb. 2010 - Vacation with siblings in La s Vegas – from left: Diane, Jeff, Mike, Stacey, Ann-Marie, and Vic

Uncle Jeff at Family Reunion 2008 – Jeff with nieces Jill, Erin and Morgan

From left: Jeff's sister Stacey, Mom, brother Vic and Jeff just after his first brain surgery

Ann-Marie, Jeff and Vic - July 2008

Jeff and his buddy Tom

Jeff and his buddy Duane a.k.a. DM

Jeff and youngest son Brett 2001 (pre-brain tumor)

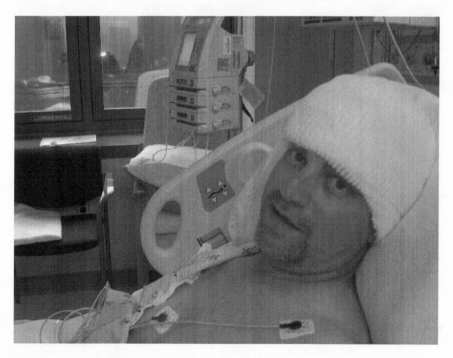

Recovery - Looking Good

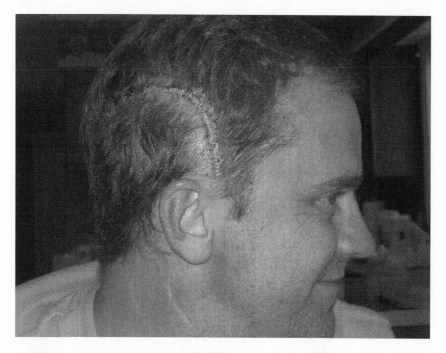

I'll show you my scar if you show me yours

Jeff's funeral – July 2009

From left: Erin, Jill, Cameron, Morgan, Brett, Amy, Patrick, and Andrew

Chapter Forty Five

The Road Trip

Posted Apr 25, 2009 8:20am

The Lord gave us a beautiful Friday yesterday with warm weather. We're hoping spring is just around the corner. My buddy Tom stopped over for a visit and Brett, Andrew and I hung out in the barn for a while chit-chatting. I enjoyed the time with them. Stacey stopped in for a visit too. Boy, aren't I the popular one? Maybe they heard that I backed off on the stool softeners and figured it was safe to stop in? When I'm on the stoolies I'm not so popular. Not sure why? Bad breath? Maybe I should chew them? Who knows?

.O.k., since the weather was nice, Diane asked if I wanted to get out of the house and take a ride in the car. We basically took the road from the house I grew up in to the house she grew up in. Yep, lots of memories. It was a nice ride. I thought Diane had the heat up too high in the car, but when she started laughing at me and pointing out what I was wearing I knew it was me. It was pushing eighty degrees outside and I had a pair of snow boots on, a winter hat, a down-filled vest, and two pairs of pants. Wow, how did I get out of the house dressed like that? Ann-Marie would have nipped that in the bud. But somehow I slipped out dressed like Nanuk of the North! Hey man looking good, or so I thought. Maybe a look-see in the mirror would have saved me some embarrassment? Diane had to tell Stacey when she came over, of course! What's a boy to do? Hey, who dressed freaky J? I don't know but how did he get out of the house? Quick, catch him before he wanders into the road........... Again!

OK back to the trip. I drove these roads a million times back in the day when Diane and I were dating in high school. We started dating when she was fifteen and I was seventeen. She had some weird "80's" hair-do thing going on! We continued our drive and had a nice talk and reminisced about the old days. We looked at the old milestones that reminded us of a different time in life. We traveled back in time but we drove in a grown up car instead of my black Trans Am. I didn't see Diane load the shovel into the trunk but the car seemed to slow down at every cemetery. She'd say, "here?" "No", I'd say "maybe the one by Mom and Dad". I think we agreed on that one for the final dirt nap. With the shovel clunking around in the trunk, did she want me to dig a hole and try it on? Lord only knows. But, we eventually made it away from the cemeteries. Hmm, creepy! If she stopped and asked, "Hey, is that a bag of trail mix", I certainly wasn't getting out to see! I'll pass, thank you. We did drive by the old houses and the memories rolled. Yes, my PMS flared up too. I was a sweaty crybaby.

We talked about family and how blessed we were. We could see how much the Lord intervened in our lives and we are very grateful for Him. We couldn't see Him so clearly then but we saw it very clear yesterday. The only thing different is, when we drove by her old house, her dad (now my wonderful father-in-law) didn't come running off the porch with his shotgun. We have a great relationship now but I didn't impress him back in the day, Yep, probably for good reason. We love each other now, Butch and I, but not so much back then. Maybe it was the ponytail and the parachute pants? Anyway, see how the Lord knew the plan? I am blessed to have Butch and Linda in my life.

O.K., the trip is over. We had a nice trip yesterday and an even greater trip since that day I caught up with her in the hallway of our high school. Thank you, Lord. Although we couldn't see Him working in our lives back then we could clearly see it yesterday. I look forward to another car ride minus the cemetery tours. If I see someone running toward the car with a shovel, I'm bailing out. But, I'm not sure how fast I can run wearing two pairs of pants and snow boots. Maybe I need to practice my driving again or learn to dress myself? Yeah, good idea.

I think my lesson yesterday was seeing how important it is to have a good relationship with God during every phase of your life. This lesson I learned for sure. The second lesson, stay off the back roads if you've had a stool softener within three to six hours. Maybe that's why Diane brought the shovel? Hmm, she's pretty smart. I guess I could have had a few handfuls of trail mix? It seems like a lifetime ago! God Bless you all – Jeff.

Chapter Forty Six

Shutting God Out

Posted Apr 27, 2009 8:31pm

Mark is a buddy of mine. We met several years ago through the motorcycle ministry I belong to. He stands about six foot four. A five foot, ten inch shrimp like me needs a brother like him to cover my back. Anyway, I didn't let him in the house the other day because I didn't recognize him when I looked through the blinds. Remember, my eyesight is still a little less than desirable these days. After he left, Diane asked, "Who was it?" I said, "I don't know but it looked like Waylon Jennings." Maybe he was checking in on me? The next day Mark and I spoke by phone and I learned it was him. That mystery was solved. I didn't let him in because I didn't recognize him.

I was wondering how many of us don't let God into our lives because we don't recognize Him? I guess to recognize Him we need to have a relationship with Him. Wow Jeff, quite a long stretch. I know, but this event was another learning point for me. I thought I would pass it on, especially after the last few days we've had around here with the strong storms and power outages.

The morning we were without electricity I was praying and let God know that I was not very happy with this situation. In fact, I was mad. I was pretty torqued off! I didn't sugar coat my prayer because I knew He already knew my heart, so I unloaded. I figured He could handle it. Today, things are much better. He sent me some helpers to get through it. My brother-in-law Mike came and fixed my fuse panel issue so my generator would keep us supplied with electricity. Since I recognized Mike I let him in. Actually, I thought it was Greg Brady for a second but it was actually Mike. So, in he comes. Thanks bro. Mike is actually my in-law but feels more like a brother. Thanks Stacey!

Later in the day my friend Duane stopped over. He is the self-appointed generator cop of the neighborhood. He makes sure everyone has gas for their generator and that it's hooked up and all that good stuff. So, he came by and checked in on us a few times. It was comforting to know he was on duty. A side note about Duane is that he races pigeons. When he first told me this I asked, "Do you still run like a girl?" I figured that the pigeons were too fast for him but he told me how it actually works. He puts a couple pigeons in a box and mails them across the country and then someone releases them and they see how long it takes for the birds to make it back to Duane's home. I can hear some guy in Iowa saying, "Who in the world keeps sending me a box of feathers and bird crap?" Hmm. That would be the same guy who gets lost in his driveway on the way to the mailbox. Just ask the birdman's wife, Jennifer. She'll tell you. Anyway, if you have Duane on your side you're blessed. Thanks D! Sorry I threw you under the bus. If we were expecting more storms tonight I might have been a little nicer to you. Sorry, but I couldn't resist the whole freaky pigeon hobby thing you got going on. Can I get a t-shirt? Oh yeah. I think I have a pigeon with a number seven crimped on his leg in my garage. After three shots with the broom he doesn't seem to have much energy to fly. Maybe he's doing chemo? You might have to pencil him in as a "no show" or should I just ship him to Iowa as is? Let me know.

Oh boy, I'm praying for good weather. I think the bird-boy might be a little mad at me. I hope Jennifer doesn't read this to him. Maybe she'll send him to check the mail. If she does, then I'll be safe. Anyway, since I recognized Duane when he came over I let him in. When he came in I had my Swine flu mask on and he sang "I'm too sexy for my mask!!" He can sure boost a guy's spirit. So, keep your door open for God to walk through and He'll bring you lots of help. Andrew knocked too. He had to, because I locked him out while he was refueling the generator in the middle of the night. Sorry! And, thanks for the help. Today I heard another knock. It was my boy Brett and his buddy. They took me for blood work. I recognized them so I let them in too. The mailman knocked too. She brought a care package from our friends (Keith & Karen) from Tennessee. Thanks for the new murse and all the thoughtful goodies! I'll fill it with the A&D ointment tomorrow! And God Bless you for the two murse sized Hanny-Sannies. I think Mark was too tall for me to see up that high so I missed the opportunity to let him in. And, I'm disappointed I missed his visit. Sorry Bro. Keep in touch and I'll see you soon.

Thanks for all your prayers and have a blessed day. Love, J

Chapter Forty Seven

Treatment and pre-pack

Posted Apr 28, 2009 5:51am

Today, Diane will take me down to the Hank for another round of chemo. It's not snowing so maybe today is not the day. No, it's today all right. I was reminded about the pre-pack when I woke up with heartburn this morning. I'll try and shed some light on the pre pack for you. I think it's a sick joke that either Doctor Roy or the chemo nurses play on me. I'll let you decide. Before my chemo treatment the nurses hang an extra I.V. bag on the pole so it can be infused before my regular chemo. They call it a pre-pack. They explain that the pre-pack has extra medicine in it to help me tolerate the chemo a little better. But, here is what I think. I think the pre-pack is a way for the nurses to play a joke on me. I am imagining in the chemo room that there is another small room off to the side with vials of liquid with the names of different side-affects on them. The nurses can pick and choose to either add the liquid to my pre-pack or not. I guess my attitude toward them helps in their decision about how much grief they wish to cause me over the next few weeks. I hope Dr. Roy doesn't prescribe the meds, especially after the comment I made about his Rickshaw. Sorry Doc!

Is Tammy back there already selecting my pre-pack meds this morning? I can see her now thinking to herself. Hmm, Jeff. Let's see…as she's grabbing the vial that will dry out my skin so I'll look like an epidermis crop duster walking through the house. Let's see. Jeff. Hemorrhoids? Yes! Weight gain. Oh for sure, she thinks. So, she adds the juice. Oh great. It sounds like a busy week for the Jeffers but she continues. Itchy butt? Definitely. Gas? You betcha! Constipation? Sure. Why not? Jeff wasn't so nice to me during his last visit so I'll kind of jack his week up a little bit. Tammy may be thinking…Constipation? Yup! That will teach him to share a coach seat on the way to Vegas with a four-pound bag of trail mix. I should have shared it with others. I will next time. Honestly! OK? Hmm. Tammy adds a little nose bleeding to the mix. And some indigestion, hair loss, PMS, and the pre-pack bag is getting bigger. I'm thinking that maybe this isn't really what is happening at the Hank but maybe the tumor is causing me to imagine this scenario. I don't know? It sounds like freaky J spewing nonsense but I'll need to find out for sure. I bet Tammy will let me know later today. Or, I'll find out next week if these physical side effects come true. I hope she doesn't think this is a wish list. I'll let you know.

Anyway, have a blessed day and I'll be praying for you all. After Tammy reads this I'll need your prayers too. Be blessed and have a great day. – Love Jeff

Chapter Forty Eight

Hiding in Plain Sight

Posted Apr 29, 2009 6:16am

The trip to the Hank for my chemo went well, especially since I'm awake and thanking God this morning for another day. A few days after Mark stopped over and I didn't let him in he told me that he could see me through the window. He told me I'm probably the worst hider he's ever seen. I told him next time I'll dive behind the couch. This is the same thing I tell my buddy Tom when he stops by and nobody is home. Tom doesn't knock real loud so we seem to miss him all the time. I tell him he knocks like a girl so now he'll call before he comes by. I wonder if hiding our true feelings is like hiding in plain sight. Or, should we always be open and honest about what we're really feeling? I do this in my prayers but do I always do it with my loved ones? I'm not saying to continually burden them but being truthful and open seems to be therapeutic. I know we shouldn't complain but I can still tell Diane what I'm feeling and I always tell God. He tells us He'll help carry our burdens.

Getting back to yesterday. We stopped for gas on the way to treatment. As I was pumping gas a funeral procession went by and all the cars had the orange magnetic flags on the roofs. I began wondering about my own funeral but quickly started laughing as the flags reminded me of a funny story. I remembered a story about hiding in plain sight. Let me explain. A few years ago, my brother-in-law's mom, Carol passed away and I took my mom to her funeral. I was taking care of Mom that day. I figured with my mom's wheelchair it would be too much work to get her to the gravesite. So, I formulated a plan. Mom and I would get into the procession of cars leaving the church but we would cut down a side street and not go to the gravesite. So, that's what we did. After we ducked out of the processional, we ran a few errands as we drove around town. Wow, this was good time management, or so I thought. As I was walking out of the Post Office there it was. We were busted. Yep, a big, orange magnetic funeral flag on the roof of my mom's van flapping in the breeze. I thought I was pretty slick ducking out of the funeral procession. But then realized we were hiding in plain sight and fooled no one. Not only did we ditch the funeral procession but it looked like I stole the funeral home's flag too. I'm sure the town's people were saying! "Hey, look at that idiot!"

So, my hiding skills have not improved. I still try to hide in plain sight and I'm sure I fool no one, especially those I love. I try not to burden them with this cancer crap I'm dealing with. But, I do let them know how much I love them and care for them and how thankful I am that they're in my life. Another day that I can see them and talk to them is a great day. I miss the old Jeff but, with the words of wisdom from Diane, I know I need to be able to enjoy the people in my path with what I have. I can still see them. I can still hear them. I can still hug them. And, I can still laugh with them. So, when I do these things, I'm no longer hiding in plain sight! Thank you, Lord.

Chapter Forty Nine

My Barn Door Was Open

Posted Apr 30, 2009 6:30am

I knew it was a rough day yesterday when I had to take my own advice. I was pretty discouraged and exhausted after this last round of chemo. When I'm tired I get discouraged because I don't have the energy to do anything. That, in turn, gets me discouraged. It's a vicious cycle. So, what does that have to do with my barn door?

Well, yesterday I heard a familiar sound, which was my lawn tractor. Ah, the sound of summer. It was Andrew. He was in the yard picking up sticks and tree limbs from the wind storm the other day. He had the tractor out and the oil changed and now we're all set for another season. As I looked out the patio window I remembered the days when he and I used to double-team that job. We'd have a few laughs along the way as we worked together. But my energy level was so low that I just watched from the kitchen window. That kind of got me depressed. As I surveyed the property I saw that Brett had the car pulled into the barn. He was doing some work on it and the two boys were going to clean the barn too. Again, a few jobs I used to do with them but didn't have the energy to go out there and hang out. I needed to rest but I really wanted to be out in the barn with my boys. My plan was to take my own advice and get out of my funk by just enjoying being able to see them, hug them, hear them and have another day with them. So, I figured I would take my own advice and do just that. There was no sense in beating myself up.

So, I prepare for my trip to the barn. First, I need to find the baby wipes and clean house, if you know what I mean. After my treatment yesterday it felt like I ate a tootsie-roll dipped in glass. I am still thinking that the pre-pack medicine had some bad stuff in it. Ouch! A baby wipe swipe and some ointment should get me to the barn easy enough. When I eventually get to the barn I stand there and cry as my PMS kicks in. "Hey, no crying in the barn" they say. They told me this is a new rule, so I comply. Then they asked, "Why are you walking funny?" "Oh, my knee is bothering me", I tell them. "Hmm, looks more like your tailbone!" I assure them that I'll be ok, but thanks for asking.

Sometimes it's good when your barn door is open except after blood work. Last week after my urine donation at the local hospital the nurse said I was free to go. So, I grabbed the door and headed out. I was feeling good until I realized my zipper was down. Yep, that barn door was definitely open. I held my murse in front of me in hopes of concealing my forgetfulness. But, I was too late. All I could do was say "oops" and zip up. "I'm a mess", I thought!

I spoke to Stacey, Vic, Ann Marie, and Duane by phone yesterday just to hear their voices. I used what I have to enjoy them…my ears. I have more calls to make today so I better get busy. I continue to pray for you all and I pray your day is blessed. Don't let it get past you. God bless you all. - Jeff

Chapter Fifty

Loose Ends

Posted May 1, 2009 5:25am

In life there always seem to be loose ends that I feel need to be tied up. It seems that everywhere I look there is something that needs to be fixed, corrected, tightened, painted, or adjusted. I know a lot of these fixes I won't be able to do myself. For some of them I'll just have to rely on the help of others I had a leaky pipe in the basement so Ken R. was my go-to-guy. Cool. Problem solved. Or, should I say, loose end tied up?

Here is what I think I learned. I'll never get all the loose ends tied up because I never have. Even the old Jeff always seemed to have something out there that he thought needed to be done, and eventually it did get done. I guess I'm telling myself this to avoid stress. It will either get done or, if it doesn't, it was probably not that big of a deal anyway!

Looking around at everything kind of reminds me of trying to take a group photograph. You finally get everyone organized and cousin Jim is missing or crazy Uncle Bud is standing by the wrong tree. It always seems to be a big production to herd everyone together. Laura, look this way. Snap. The picture is taken. Now, let me see it. Oh no. John has his eyes closed. I knew he was hanging around the keg too long. Jim has red eye, at least in the one he has open. What in the world is on Uncle Jim's head? Is it Jeff's murse? Uncle Fred's zipper is down. Aunt Jane looks mad at Susan. Joe has his mouth open, nothing new here. The Debbies are facing away from the camera. Mike is kneeling down so now we can't see him. Who was watching him? Mike looks like he's posing for a mug shot. Uncle Pete has some strings hanging from his shorts. Oh wait… those are his legs. Shannon is laughing again. So, all we see are teeth. Aunt Judy, Mimi and Jackie look like they are ready to arm wrestle. Matt, Griff, and Uncle Vic are facing the wrong way. Katy, more red eye. Who told Uncle Jerry to do the thumbs up? Couldn't he see Andrew, Brett, and Tom doing the one thumb pose? Now he's blocking Vic's face. Hmm, maybe that was the plan? Joe? Yep, muscleman poses, just like all the photos from the last nine years. Who was in charge of him this year? Rosa? Fixing her hair. It's a little windy out here. Jeff? Looking for something in his murse, probably some hand sanitizer. He must have thought that someone made some incidental contact with him. Chris and Scott? Who knows? They look like a singing group with the matching tank tops. By the way, who dressed Mike this year? There's Mary yawning or screaming at someone. Who knows? Stacey (Octo mommy) is missing. Probably rounding someone up? Liz is pointing at Katy. Who knows why? Who made her the photo cop?

OK, we botched another attempt to get a group photo. Why should this one be any different from our last attempt? Some of the names have been changed to protect the innocent. But, here is the bottom line. Just when you think you have all the loose ends identified and a fix planned for them, you'll find something else that's not right. So, don't fret. Everything will work out for the best if it's God's plan. It always does. Also, realize that you'll never have it all together, kind of like trying to take a group photo.

Hang your toilet paper
Posted May 1, 2009

Hanging toilet paper is another phrase for being prepared. You can't wait until you go to reach for the cushy tube to realize it's not there. When you hit the bathroom door you've got to be on your game and assess the situation. If you have to shuffle around with your drawers around your ankles, it's too late. You've got to have the roll hanging. Be prepared. I try to apply this in my own life with my relationship with God. I've said it a thousand times and I'll say it again. I don't know how anyone can go through some fatal disease like cancer without being able to lean on God. I still have my good and bad days but, right now, I feel my relationship with God is rock solid. I talk with Him all day long. I give Him thanks for all He has given me. I even get angry with Him when I'm having a bad.day. But, the key point is that I have ongoing dialog with Him through prayer all day long.

I'm not saying I'm not ready to go to heaven right now but my toilet paper is hanging and I'll be there when He's ready for me. I still don't know His plan for my life so I still have hope that this chemo will do the job. He may need me on this earth a little bit longer to check the toilet paper holders. Only He knows. Oh man.

Easter – Jesus Christ was born of a virgin, died on a cross for our sins, was buried, and rose again. You know about Easter. If you truly believe, you will be saved and go to heaven.

This gives me great comfort to know where I'm going when I checkout from this hotel of life. I have great comfort in knowing this.

So, get your paper hanging. Be prepared!

May God bless you. I'm on a roll. Or, at least sitting next to a full one!!!! – Jeff.

Chapter Fifty One

Tough Day

Posted May 1, 2009 1:32pm

I'm looking at this day as a reminder day. I'm being reminded of the good days I have. Today is not so good, lots of frustrations. I know the reason is that I'm tired, which amplifies each little issue. I say little issue because that's what they are. I can't get the kitchen drawer closed and it makes me want to jump out of my skin. I dropped a whole bunch of cereal on the floor and I know it will be a matter of time before I'm crunching it beneath my stinky slippers. The crunch sound, I know, will cause me to freak out. This mild headache isn't helping matters either. The sunshine is nice but I can't enjoy it because I'm fixated on the cereal on the floor. I can see little bacteria guys standing around it waiting to carry them off to their den. I guess I don't want to know. Today, Diane is running to some appointments but I'm too exhausted to tag along with her. I used to like tagging along with her because we always had a good time just spending time together. But today I'll have to sit it out. She understands.

I'm still hopeful that those days will return. I still don't know the Lord's plan for me, or for us?

Today, I think the Lord's plan is to remind me to appreciate the good days. I know every day won't be this bad. Today is kind of a burr-under-the-saddle day. I guess I needed it but I sure don't want it. I call it a jump-out-of-my-skin day! That seems to apply better. There is a bump on every road I've been on today. Andrew and Brett just came in. I said, "Tell me some good news." They said they didn't have any. But it got us talking and I'm feeling much better. I thanked them for bringing me some sunshine. Jesus must have sent them. You know what? I think I'll be OK! Thanks for this day! They cleaned up my cereal catastrophe! Now I can relax because the germ dudes won't be molesting the Captain Crunch that was lying all over the floor. Life is good. Life IS good! Amen! Freaky J will make it! ;)

Chapter Fifty Two

Care Package

Posted May 3, 2009 7:20am

An old neighbor of ours from Tennessee sent us a care package the other day. Let me back up. She's not old in the birthday sense of the word. We have just known her for a while. One of the gifts she sent was a new murse with pictures of motorcycles on it. I love it. When I take a break after a long hard ride I'll have a place to carry my pumps or lip gloss, depending on the ride. The last time I wore my pumps I burned my ankle on the exhaust… and got beat up! I couldn't run fast enough in the pumps!

Where am I going with this? Well, here it is. When stuff is in my murse you can't see it. When you look at me you sometimes don't always see everything either. I'm like an egg. I have a hard shell on the outside but I'm gooey on the inside. My heart and emotions are all gooey. The shell is a natural growth after years of living. The shell protects my insides and can seem to only get harder with each life experience. The gooey yoke just sloshes around but is protected by the shell. I think you get the picture. I realized my PMS flare-ups are found somewhere within the yoke part. My dry, itchy, chemo skin is found on the shell. The constipation, bloody noses, shaky hands, dry mouth, not sure. But, the list can go for miles.

Here is what I want to say. Without prayer my shell would crack. So, I am mindful to pray continually and I want to thank you all again for your prayers. I am returning the favor to you all daily.

Have a blessed day. – From the egg man!

Chapter Fifty Three

Lighten Up

Posted May 4, 2009 7:00am

I would consider yesterday a good day, if you call being tired, shuffling around the house, and crying a good day. If not, I would chalk another one up to a bad day. I guess the day was a little bit of both with the fatigue seeming to get the upper hand. I think my PMS and the accompanying tears added to the frustration. The weather was great but I was not feeling up to going to my niece, Erin's birthday party. This always puts a little stress on me. I want to do something but don't have the energy to do it. I know that everyone understands, but it doesn't make it any easier to accept. I guess that's the key word here, accept.

Do what you can do is what I tell myself. People will understand. They usually do. I mean, how couldn't they? Would you want me hanging around your party? You would have to keep me from touching the grill and drinking out of the dog dish. Up goes the pool safety fence, Jeff's here. Oh for crying out loud, get him to the bathroom. Who's watching him? Jeff, you've had too much Kool-Aid. Come on, get in the house. Where's his murse? I need the wipes. Well, maybe my visit wouldn't play out like that but who knows? Note to self: put clean shorts in the murse just in case one pair of the normal two pairs get wet. Who needs to organize any entertainment at a party anymore? Just invite Freaky J and let him wander around for an hour or two. If the crying jags don't entertain the crowds just wait until he has a full bladder. Hmm. Good times had by all.

Erin's party may not have gone this bad but, when Freaky J's in the hood, you never know. Maybe my mind is working overtime this morning. Maybe we'll just send a card this year. And, maybe Diane will let me sign my own name? FfeJ, instead of using the infamous "X". We'll see if I'm holding the pencil properly. The last time I tried she had to pry it out of my hand and reposition it. I think I'm learning. The "X" is easier and it makes for a good conversation starter. Aw, good job. Look!

I prayed for a good message for this blog entry this morning. Being able to laugh at myself was the answer I received. I think the Lord knew that I needed to lighten up, especially after yesterday. So, maybe not taking myself so seriously is the theme here. It seems to be helping so I'm going to run with it. Happy Birthday E, I hope it was nice. I love you.

Have a blessed day. To everyone: Laugh at yourself at least once. A good belly laugh does the spirit good and seems to reduce the stress levels. Remember, no one is perfect. If you can't find anything funny about yourself just ask someone. I'm sure they could find something. But, if you ask, be prepared for any answer and don't take it too personally. OK? God Bless!! – Jeff.

Chapter Fifty Four

Swine Flu

Posted May 5, 2009 6:18am

As a kid growing up in rural Michigan my dad always seemed to have pigs and chickens on the farm. I think the most we had at one time was about sixty-four pigs, which kept us busy feeding them and cleaning the stalls. Come to think of it, Dad never mentioned anything about catching the swine flu. Had I known, I might have been able to catch an extra couple of days off from school or ditch out from a chore or two. But, you know Dad. "You're young," he would say, which meant you'll be ok! I guess he was right but I never asked what the cut-off age was for being young. I wish I knew now. Come to think of it he never mentioned the bird flu either. Was he trying to kill us? Maybe, but we were young!

I was watching the news and I saw that there are several hundred deaths worldwide from this current swine flu problem. Somehow they think they have it narrowed down to "patient zero." That would be the first pig to have the flu and the one blamed with passing it on. Hmm, interesting. Anyway, it's interesting how this flu has spread from one lousy pig. OK., maybe he's not lousy just unlucky. This flu has found itself affecting many countries and many people just by human-to-human contact. If that doesn't activate my freak-o-meter then the people on TV won't either. Seeing the people with the masks on is a little unnerving but I'm hanging in there. My mask and me fit right in now. I pray that they get this pandemic under control. They have in the past so I'm sure they can again.

Seeing how this flu has traveled around the world from a small farm in Mexico is a good reminder to us of how we can affect so many people just by one little contact. Just think if we did one small but kind deed for someone and they did the same for the next person? Our single good deed would be multiplied a thousand times. Hmm, looks like a good return on your investment, unless you pass along the flu. Other than that it would be a good investment. Think about this. Maybe when you're holding the door open for someone at the store today you'll really be holding it open for yourself tomorrow. So, don't fart in a crowded elevator! Can you dig that? My mom would say, "Be kind to others before they're kind to you." Very good advice I would say. Bless someone today. Love Jeff

Chapter Fifty Five

Ask And You Shall Receive

Posted May 6, 2009 7:04pm

I'm sure this Bible verse is familiar to you. I use it in my daily prayers. I ask for healing and sometimes I just ask for understanding or patience or help. The key, I think, is to just ASK. And, believe He will answer your need. One thing that I have learned through my illness is that if you need something you must ask for it. People are not mind readers but they are always willing to help. Like yesterday, Tom drove me to my blood work appointment and was willing to hold my urine cup during that part of the appointment. But, I didn't ask. I figured he would be laughing so hard that his shaky hand would dump the contents all over my pants. I guess some things are better left alone. I wonder if I just caught my last ride with Tom?

I was thinking about the days when my dad was still alive. I keep thinking how I wish I would have done this or done that for him when he was still here. Then it dawned on me that I would have but I didn't know. He never asked. He was a private person and most times kept things to himself. For me, it seems easier to give to someone than to receive. But lately I do more asking. This has been a good lesson in humility for me. I am grateful that I have a good network of helpers. Everyone that has ever been mentioned in these pages has been there for Diane and me without fail. I just needed to ask. Would Tom hold the urine cup? I guess I'm not sure on that one. All right, I'm sure he would tell me I'm on my own. I'll cut him a break on this one. I guess the key is this. If you need something, ask.

May the Good Lord bless you all and I'll be back, if the good Lord is willing.

Chapter Fifty Six

Shockproof

Posted May 7, 2009 7:18am

Yesterday I was talking with my cousin Scott about these blog entries I have been posting. I told him how some of them have been used in Bible studies. I explained that I pray that God uses each entry and that it reaches the right person at the right time with the right message. I do this for each entry and I definitely try and stay out of the way. I also commented to Scott that I know some of these entries may be a little raunchy for a Christian Bible study. But, as adults, we should be able to handle the content. I then wondered how a poopy roadside bathroom key stick could be used for His message, or the body condom, or some poor soul holding a urine cup? Waxed bullets, constipation, stool softeners, and the list of non-traditional teaching aids grow. How are these items used to convey the message of salvation through Jesus Christ? Hmm, I wonder? And, what's the deal with the four pounds of trail mix and Nurse Bob's removal procedure? I often wonder how a Bible study progresses through these sensitive topics but I think we figured it out.

We need to be shockproof because most people won't open a Bible to read the Word. But, they will watch you. You, as a Christian may be the only Bible they know. So, I think it's important to be real and not too righteous.

A few years ago I received and completed some Chaplain training with my Biker buddy, Ten Spot. The certification doesn't make you a better Christian or give you a stronger faith in God. But, it did provide us with the credentials to enter areas like jails and hospitals to conduct Bible studies. Just because you have a piece of paper calling you a Chaplain doesn't make you a super-Christian. It only gives you a piece of paper that helps open doors that would normally be closed to you. Kind of like a driver's license. Just because you have one it doesn't make you a better driver. Can you dig that? Anyway, the first door that opened was a minimum-security jail where a few of us (Tenspot, Mark a.k.a.Waylon, Rick, and myself) held a weekly Bible study with the inmates. It was a nice time but you never were sure what you would see or hear. You had to be shockproof. You had to be mature enough to not freak out or panic if they said some crude things. They were just testing us to find out if we were real Christians. Could they weed out the weak? This was where having a relationship with Christ was important and not just belonging to a religion. Remember, the religious guys were the ones who crucified Christ. Having a strong relationship with Him, with Jesus, is your best defense. Sometimes that's easier said than done. But, we are all works in progress, as Mom would say.

Being shockproof is nothing less than being real. If we think being a Christian means you can't laugh or joke around we are mistaken. You should let your heart lead you if you truly have a relationship with "J.C." Nobody is perfect except God himself! AND, He has a good sense of humor too. Why else would he allow me to go out in public with two pair of pants (one hole included), snow boots, a knit hat, and my fly open? He knew someone needed a good laugh and he knew I could handle it. The pants were corduroy for added warmth during those eighty-degree days. I really get warm in them when Diane has me digging with that shovel she keeps in the trunk. Is a six-foot deep garden a little unusual? I'll have to ask Cheryl or Todd. It seems a little deep?

I pray that this blog meets you with wisdom. May God bless your day and God bless all those you meet today. Come to know Christ AS YOU ARE. There is no need to get cleaned up first. No shower needed. I say AMEN to that!

-Love Jeff

Been there. Done it!

May 8 2009

I was looking at some old photographs the other day and remembering back to the time they were taken. And, I was trying to think about what I remembered of that day. One photo shows Diane, Andrew, Brett and I sitting in a jeep in the sand dunes. I remembered it was a fun day and I really enjoyed our time that day, even the lunch and the ice cream we had. It reminded me of a time when I felt better and probably looked better too. Could there have been a time when I looked better? Hmm. I just checked the mirror and I think the answer to that question is "yes." The mirror doesn't lie, does it?   Who is the moon faced dude looking back at me? Hey, the dry skin around my nose is a nice touch and the big old gut looks kind of sexy. If I just lost a little bit more hair I would be all set. Maybe Nurse Tammy can set me up with that during her next pre-pack concoction before my next treatment? Sure she will. I bet I won't even have to ask her.

Anyway, as I was saying, I remember the photo and how much better I was feeling and how much better I was looking too. Then, as I was looking at the photo, I had this thought. Was I enjoying the moment at the time the photo was taken? Was I taking it all in or was I in a funky mood? Did I smell the roses? I'm sure I said, "Hey, who's cutting the roses", and I'm sure I had to yell at the boys a time or two. But, that's part of being a dad I guess? "Hey, quit spitting. Keep your hands inside the jeep. Turn the radio down. You're just going to have to hold it!" You know the typical banter! I wish I could hear it now!

Here is my point. If I took a picture of myself today and looked at it in a few years, would I say, "Wow, that was a good day?" I felt good but did I really enjoy that day? So, reflecting on the photo I took today, would I remember the good things that happened and say, "Hey, that was a better time?" I hope so.

Brett just came in from work so I got to see him and that is a good part of my day. Andrew came in a little bit earlier too. I see the sunshine. Diane will be home from the grocery store in a few minutes. I would hope that if I look at a photo of me taken today, but only a few moments ago, that I would remember the good things from that day. You know, I could look at it and say that I've been there and done that. Or, do I sit in a tired funk and look for the bad things of today? Nope. I am choosing to look at the good.

Chapter Fifty Seven

Let Your Yes Be Yes

Posted May 8, 2009 6:49am

Yesterday I was reminded of this Bible verse while visiting with my friend, DM. I'll use his initials to cut him a little slack on this one. In a quick summary, the verse tells us how important our word should be to someone as well as to ourselves. When we are asked a question our answer should really be a simple "yes" or "no." It should also be something that the other person can believe in and trust without fail, every time. In today's world we seem to need contracts, signatures, thumbprints, etc. But, what we all really need is each other's word. That's it. So, let your "yes" be "yes" and your "no" be "no." I hope I don't sound like I'm on a high horse because I'm certainly not without fault. But, this verse is something that I've learned over the years and was one of the first verses I remembered as a new Christian. It's very memorable to me and my visit with DM reminded me of it.

DM stopped by the house for a visit to see if the light cover he has will be able to replace the broken one that I have. We do a quick check in the barn to see and then we sit in the garage and talk for a few minutes. Unfortunately, I can't concentrate on a single word he is saying. When he crossed his leg I see that the bottom of his left shoe is full of dog crap. As I fixate on it I see that it's all mashed into the tread and everything. Oh, what to do? My anti-bacteria alarm was screaming a code blue. What if he wants to go inside the house? Does it smell? What's he going to do? What should I do? Hmm, I need to let him know, was my first thought. I say, "Hey, you have some dog poop on the bottom of your shoe." But then he threw me a curve ball. He looks down at it and says "No I don't." What? Is this guy for real? He just looked at it and that's his best answer? I said "Sure there is." "No, it's sand from your barn" he says. Huh? Is this guy for real? So he does the next logical thing. He pops his shoe off and smells it. Then he's in the driveway doing some kind of jig to scrub the alleged poop from his shoe. Great, now I can step in it later too. Here is this guy denying the poop and I can see it plain as day. So, the next time we're out of dog food I'll just give it a bowl of sand? Is that what the crazy guy who's dancing in my driveway is telling me?

Well, I survived this stressful ordeal and learned that he was right. So, for good reason, his no was no. It sure looked like poop but maybe things aren't always what they appear to be. DM reminded me of one of my early verses. I know I'll always be able to trust his word. Thanks Bro! Have a blessed day. My barn door will always be open. Well, you know what I mean.

God Bless and thanks for everything. - Jeff.

Chapter Fifty Eight

Pick Your Battles

Posted May 9, 2009 7:32am

This was something that our mom would always tell my sisters and me when we began to have children of our own. She would say, "Pick your battles." Basically, she knew that when children reach a certain age a battle would be looming at every corner. She was telling us to not enter into every battle but be selective. Hopefully you'll enter a battle that you have a chance to win. That was her underlying objective. I'm glad that Mom had the wisdom to pick her battles with me. Yes, I think back and believe that I usually lost the battle but I gained a lot of wisdom along the way. Ok, maybe I could have left out the phrase "a lot". I surely don't have a lot of wisdom and I can prove it. At least that's what my buddy Walter would say.

I think this phrase can apply in every area of our lives, not just with our kids. We could apply this in our church, our neighborhood, our job, and everywhere in between. Yes, I think that was her point. Church? For real? Well, I think so because churches are made up of people and we all seem to have a hard time leaving our burdens at the door. Some days we're probably dressed for battle. My battle clothes look like this; two pair of pants, one pair with a hole in it exposing my undies, and a pair of boots that are unseasonably out of style. A knit hat and a sweatshirt to insure I bead-up and sweat profusely, which is why they seem to save me a seat on the sinner's bench. Sir, sit here, we saved you a seat. Hmm. I'll definitely let that battle go unchallenged. You never know what the crazy dude with the swine flu mask will do. Hey, don't stare at him. He might flip out. Does he think he's a super-hero in training or just a germ freak? Uh-oh, he's walking this way. Quick, cut your eyes to the left and maybe he'll leave you alone. He looks ready for battle. Just look at what he's wearing. Aren't those boots hot and what's that smell? Is that sand or dog poop on the sole of his shoe? It looks like poopy sand to me.

I know that when you pick your battles you probably have a better chance at winning. Ah ha, maybe that was Mom's point? Keep the peace, do some teaching and learn something about yourself along the way. Ok, I relearned this lesson again and hopefully you all can take away a small piece of it and apply it in your own lives.

Have a blessed week and watch where you step. – I love you all- Jeff.

Chapter Fifty Nine

Let Go and Let God

Posted May 11, 2009 8:13am

This was a saying that I recall my mom always telling me. Maybe it is appropriate that I remembered it on Mother's Day! I'm not surprised. I'm sure the Lord had His hand in it. This is still one area that I seem to struggle with on a daily basis, but hopefully today may be different. I'm up at 3AM and I'll tell you why. The boys are getting ready to leave for work and someone is drying some clothes in the dryer. But, I think they added a couple of coins or rocks to the dryer. It's NOISY. It reminds me of someone drying a pair of bib-over-alls with all the straps and snaps. So I'm awake. The good news is that I was able to see the dudes before they headed out to work. Uh oh. I just remembered. Tom will be taking me in for some blood work in a few hours.

You know what that means? Yep. Big Jeff needs to take a shower. Well, I'm probably due for one anyway. I'll clean up or maybe I'll just wear the stinky slippers and blame any stinkage on them. NO! I will shower today. Ok that's settled! Whew! It's too early in the morning to argue with myself.

As I move down life's time line I still find myself getting a little stressed about things that I feel are still left opened, undone, or unfinished. You would think this would be the least of my worries. But, something always seems to pop up. It's kind of strange. I remember that I have a great support system so I shouldn't sweat it. Things are getting done. "Hey Jibs, the grass looks good!" And, "Thanks Mike for dropping in the new sump pump." Thanks for yesterday. I love you and Stacey!

I think I just found out what that extra pill was that Diane gave me yesterday. Yep. I think it was a stoolie! I need to make sure I don't try and pass some gas because I could have a mess on my hands. Well, I guess it wouldn't be on my hands but you know what I mean. Note to self, chalk-type pills are safer. The Glycerin-type pills I need to be careful of. I know that I need to step back and let the Lord into the driver's seat so he can take over. He does a better job than I do, as you all know. I am trusting that He will see me through this time in my life and I am not worried. I trust Him and I know He has a perfect plan for my family and me. Sometimes we may have to walk in the valley but at least we're still walking. And, He's right there with us. So Lord, today I thank you for everything and I'll allow you to lead the way. I'll let go and let you! You know it's easier for me to say it than to do it but I will keep working on it... with your help.

Mike, the new sump pump makes my eyes water when I hear it running. Maybe it's broken. No. I think it's my PMS flaring. I love you water boy! Thanks!

In closing, the real message here is not about worrying about the sump pump but turning our children (no matter what age) over to God to let Him mold them in the way He wants them. And, to keep them on the path He has set for them. So, that's where I'm trying to let go and let Him!

Chapter Sixty

Objects In Mirror Are Closer Than They Appear

Posted May 12, 2009 6:54am

Having a good accountability partner. I always wonder if we see things as they really are or do we only think we do? Kind of like the dog crap I saw on DM's shoe the other day. It was a good thing he (DM) snapped off his shoe and smelled it or I would still be thinking it was the real deal. I was reminded that maybe I don't always see things as they really appear. When the telephone rang today I grabbed it. "Hello, hello, hello" I repeated. Hmm, must be a prank call. I bet one of the Hank valet dudes found a loose number in my car's console and is dialing away trying to disrupt some lives! I knew that would happen soon enough. Anyway, as I go to hang up the phone I realize the phone, which used to be black, is now yellow. Dang! I answered a banana, a cordless banana. No wonder I couldn't hear anyone.

I guess this tells me that my eyesight on the left is still gone. I thought the phone felt squishy when I answered it. So, what I thought I saw was something entirely different.

I think I woke up with a new side affect this morning. It felt like my entire sinus pool drained into my throat at one time. I woke up coughing and gagging and hustled to the kitchen. It was a good thing I didn't need to call 911. They probably would have connected me to Charo. You know, Whoochy Koochy! I could have been in big trouble. But I guess since I'm still here, no damage was done. Then, the highlight of my day came next. Yeah! BM time. That's medical speak for purging the pipeline. Again, I was reminded of a candy bar dipped in glass. Another joke my body is playing on me.

Needless to say, my murse and its endless supply of countermeasures would have something to fix me up, like a skin colored patch, ointment, and a real bullet to bite down on. Anyway, it will all come out in the end.

Chapter Sixty One

Another Field Trip – Blood Work

Posted May 13, 2009 5:24am

The other day I blogged about letting go and letting God. I woke up this morning and it took me about twelve seconds to blow it. But, I recovered quickly. I do learn, albeit slowly. I guess that's better than not learning at all! My buddy Tom took me for my blood work appointment yesterday. Looking back, I enjoyed the day with him. After the appointment we went down to the river and had lunch. We watched a few ships make their way downriver to destinations unknown. We sat and talked and just enjoyed each other's company. We talked a little about everything. We talked about the past, the future and a little about the day. After he got me back home the routine was about the same. He drops me off, I cry, and he heads out. He knows it's the

PMS so there is no need to explain my crying episodes. This makes saying goodbye and thank you a lot easier. Thanks Tom. I love you. Tom was glad that he didn't have to hold my urine cup during the dreaded fill up. So, I think it was a good day for him too. I brought him some hand sanitizer just in case. Tom and I have done a lot in the past so I'm hopeful we'll still be able to squeeze in a few more outings. Thanks for your help today Tom. I'll be in touch and may God bless you as he has me with your friendship.

I love you. Jeff.

Chapter Sixty Two

Being Quiet

Posted May 13, 2009 5:51pm

Lately, the fatigue has really been tough on me. I'm not sure if it's the medicine or my poor sleeping patterns. It's probably a combination of both. My brother Vic is in town for a visit so it was nice seeing him. I was able to show him how fast I can cry, thanks to my new PMS. He seemed pretty impressed and said I should look into becoming a Soap opera star since I can cry at the drop of a hat. I'm not sure if people really cry when you drop a hat but I bet I will before the end of the week! Hopefully my head won't be in the hat when I drop it.

I woke up early today and just sat quietly on the couch and prayed and listened. You would think with two ears and one mouth that I would listen twice as much as I speak. But, I seem to talk more than I listen. So, sitting quietly was a nice change. I think I'll do it more often. I should plan more quiet time to just sit with those I love. That's it. Just sit with them and listen. I guess an occasional word or two would come up but I would really focus on listening. This would include listening to God too. The quiet of this morning was so nice. I usually have so much junk bouncing around in my head that I just can't seem to get a moment of peace. I can imagine how the people in my life feel. Hmm, is that Jeff talking again? Did you ever listen to a tape recording of your own voice? When I hear my voice I say, "That doesn't sound like me. Gross turn it off. Do I really sound like that? Oh, that's awful. I sound weird." That alone is enough motivation to do more listening and less talking. That will be one of my goals. Enjoy quiet time and listen, listen, listen.

Have a great day. I won't talk to you later but I will be listening.

Be blessed.
Love Jeff

Treatment

Posted May 14, 2009

On Tuesday Diane and I embarked for another road trip to the Hank for treatment. I wonder why they call it treatment because some days it doesn't seem like much of a treat. But, I guess it's necessary. I guess the biggest treat is that we get a chance to see the nurses and have a few laughs with them, which is always nice. Those queens of chemo always take good care of us. Their jobs are demanding and stressful but they always seem to keep it together and I'm grateful to call them friends.

Here is a recap of the day. As soon as we pull into the main gate I see the all too familiar red jacket valet guys and I immediately begin to gather up any loose change in the car and stick it in to my pocket. After I do a thorough cabin search of the car we surrender the keys and dash to the front door of hospital. I ask Diane, "Where's my murse?" "It's in your hand," she answers. So, I guess we're good to go. "Where's your purse? Do you have your purse?" I'll repeat this a few times and we eventually reach the elevator and wait for it to bring a whole group of sick folks into my life. After the doors open we squeeze in and hope the poor soul we're standing next to isn't as sick as he looks. But at this point, it's like rolling the dice. But this time was a little different.

The dude behind me was whistling along with the music they were piping into this box of horror and, ironically enough, the song was "All I need is the air that I breathe." I could imagine his air was causing my zone to get funky. But I felt ok because I was wearing my swine flu mask. I was really wishing I had a body condom on. I was pretty happy when the doors opened at the thirteenth floor. I bolted to the check in desk, after a brief stop at the hand sanitizer station, for a quick scrub down. Whew, I made it! And after a brief wait, they came and got me and found me a chair so I could begin my IV drip. Vic met us in the Chemo room. It was nice to have him there.

Tammy stopped by my chair and said she put a little something extra in my pre-pack. I guess I'll find out what special side affect she has planned for me later today. Hmm, I can't wait to find out. I know that she really doesn't pick a special bag of side affects for me but it's fun to laugh about it.

As I was getting ready for bed I shouted out, "Bloody nose!" I told Diane I found out what Tammy selected for my pre-pack side affect and we had a good laugh. I was glad she didn't select runny stool with gas. I can deal with the bloody nose. Thanks T. At least I can still eat trail mix with a bloody nose. If the mix binds me up I'll be sure to come and see you.

Chapter Sixty Three

The Old Bus Route

Posted May 16, 2009 9:29am

Thursday, the warm weather encouraged me to want to get out of the house. I asked Andrew if he wanted to get some lunch and take a ride. Brett was working so it would just be Andrew and me. I was hoping to drive but I didn't feel I was up to it yet. Andrew manned the wheel. We dropped off some mail at the post office, grabbed a sandwich, and then just decided to drive around. I didn't have an agenda but my goal was to just sit with him and enjoy his company. We didn't talk much but just sitting with him was nice. More quiet time with someone I love. Brett will be in the car on my next trip I'm sure. As we drove the back roads, we ended up on the same route that my school bus took when I wore a younger man's clothes! As we drove, I would point out a few useless facts and reminisce. No lectures, so I know that Andrew was thankful for that. We just sat and connected without having to say a whole lot. We just spent some nice quiet time together.

I'll keep this entry short because the fatigue over the past few days has really wore me out. I'll catch up later. I just wanted to let you know that I'm working on keeping up with my quiet time and enjoying the special folks in my life. I know I don't always have to be saying something but just sitting quietly and taking it all in. Have a blessed day and I'll be praying for you too.

Thanks and God Bless.

Chapter Sixty Four

Jeffrey

Posted May 19, 2009 2:57pm

I'm sorry to disappoint everyone but this isn't Jeff. It's just me, Diane. Jeff has been pretty worn out so I thought I would fill in for him until he feels better. Stacey picked Jeff up this morning for his blood work and they are still out. So, hopefully that means he's feeling better. They've been gone awhile. Jeff always comes home with a story after a field trip with Stacey, usually about her driving.

I was noticing all the magnets that cover our refrigerator and I noticed four in particular. They have been a part of our refrigerator for many years. On these magnets are our names and the meaning of our names. I was reading Jeff's and it is more meaningful now then when I first read it. I thought I'd share it with you.

Jeffrey

Meaning: 'Peace'

Jeffrey has extraordinary coping skills.
His good name is his most precious asset.
Loyalty and sincerity are his dominating
qualities. His motto is 'Take the initiative,
be bold!' His study skills are the key to a
good education. Destined for greatness,
nothing can hold back this gifted person.

Not even a brain tumor has changed the qualities that make
Jeff, Jeff!

Well, Jeff made it home in one piece and I told him I
was blogging for him. Of course he cried and thanked me. I
told him, "You blog, I'll stick to being the boss!" ☺

Chapter Sixty Five

Intervention?

Posted May 21, 2009 11:58am

The other day when Diane and my sisters were talking I thought I heard my name and the word intervention mentioned in the same sentence. I figured I was in trouble. Yep, O' Jeff was being triple-teamed by Ann-Marie, Stacey & my lovely wife. It seemed that they thought I needed a shower. Again? I mean, how many showers does a boy need? With the nice weather we're having I could easily go another week or two? Hmm. Maybe three? I remember when my Dad was sick I had the same discussion with him too. "Hey Dad, I think you need a shower. Are you ready Mr. Stinky?" It takes a lot of energy to take a shower and I think that is why, when someone is sick, it's harder to keep them motivated to keep up on the showers. This seems to be the case with me. I've always showered a couple times a day but lately it's getting a lot tougher. When I can begin to smell myself maybe I'll be ready. If I look in my murse, I'm sure I can find some mentholated ointment to put it in my nose. I should be able to go another two weeks. Easily! I think the CSI guys do this trick. Hey, It's worth a try. And look how much energy I could save. Not to mention time. I see an opportunity to invent a new car smell for soap-challenged folks. New guy smell! Hmm, another million dollar idea perhaps?

Ok, if I don't sit on a wooden chair and I keep my legs together I think I could keep on living with the baby-wipes. Yeah. This may be my new clean up method. Plus, I could keep going with the two pair of pants too. They would act as a filter and keep my funk from reaching mainstream air. I think the possibilities are endless as to how I could cut back on the showers. Look how much time and money I could save? I would lose some friends along the way but I think they would understand what I'm going through.

I guess I should force their hand and wait for the intervention. I'll wait and see how long I can hold out. Hmm, I'll keep you posted on my progress and I'll smell you later. Remember, when you come to Jesus you don't need to get cleaned up first. Just come as you are and He'll clean you up.

May the Lord bless you all. I hope to see you all soon and I hope I'm not too gamey! I would hate for the word to get to the street that Jeff smells pretty rank. Sir stink-a-lot will sign out. Have a blessed day!

With the nice break in the weather I've been thinking that it would be nice to get to Tennessee to visit my mother and father in-law. I always enjoy visiting Butch and Linda and always get plenty to eat. My brother in law and sister in law are there too. One nice thing about visiting them is it's a pretty much come as you are event. When you run into my mother in-law in a bathrobe at the grocery store you'll figure it out pretty quickly. It reminds me of my relationship with God. I can pretty much come as I am. I don't need to get cleaned up, just come as I am. He'll clean me up later!

I'll keep this entry short as I'm already running out of energy to type. I'm hoping to catch up on a little sleep and catch up on some of my writings. So, I'm relying on your prayers to help me through. I'll be in touch if the good Lord is willing, and I'll continue to keep you all in my prayers. I'll be in touch and may God bless you all. Love Jeff

Chapter Sixty Six

Retro Toy

Posted May 24, 2009 8:00am

We were talking the other day and got on the subject of this child-hood toy. This popular toy is shaped like a head but is supposed to be a potato. Do you remember it? Its butt was hinged so you could stow his eyes, hats, legs and arms, etc. I believe there was a syringe and a crack pipe that came with him and his disguises too! Who came up with the idea behind this toy? Could someone hide some trail mix in his booty? HE HAD A LOT OF JUNK IN HIS TRUNK! It sure would be a lot easier to get it out in case it became lodged in there. I'm sure that's what Bob the nurse would say?

I guess the point here is what do we choose when we're selecting our parts? Do we choose our angry eyes or happy eyes? Do we choose a frown or a smile? Do we dig around and put in our lovey eyes? The choice is up to us. I have my PMS eyes in right now but I'll change them out and put in my happy eyes, and then my eyes of faith. They smile!

Chapter Sixty Seven

The Stabbing

Posted May 25, 2009 9:04am

Yesterday, Diane gave me a little excitement or maybe a little stress would be a better word. It happened at lunchtime as she was cutting an avocado for her hamburger. When we were visiting her Aunt Diane in Texas a few months back, her aunt showed her a foolproof method to remove the pit. My Diane obviously wasn't paying close attention during the lesson. I was sitting at the snack bar as Diane was jabbing and prying at the avocado pit with a knife in the hopes of getting the pit out. The words 'that doesn't look like a good idea' just rolled off my tongue but it was too late. YEP, a self-inflicted wound in her palm was the result. I shuffled around getting her some fruit, milk, water, and other non-medical aids to keep her from passing out. I was the only one home with her and not able to drive her to the clinic for stitches. Luckily, her sister Donna was close by and agreed to stop by and drive her to the doctor's. THANKS sis.

As she's getting ready to leave I start to get worried. What if the hospital thinks her cut is a defensive wound from some knife-wielding maniac? Would the next knock on my door be the SWAT takedown team looking to do some chalk drawings on my kitchen floor? Since I was wearing my usual extra set of clothing, would I look like a flight risk? Since I was wearing the winter boots I probably wouldn't need any leg irons. But, in the hot police car the shower issue might come up. Hey, they could just mace me down and maybe that would hide my funky smell. Two squirts please. I could blame the odor on the slippers!

Well, no one ever came looking to slap the cuffs on me so I think I'm safe for the time being. I'm thankful that Diane was able to get patched up and I'm able to sleep in my own bed. As she said, it could have been worse. I could be sitting on the Group-W bench munching on some trail mix with Hollis awaiting my trial. We're praying for a fast recovery and healing. Thank you Lord. When they speak of the double-edged sword in scriptures we know what He means. Thanks for your prayers and have a blessed day.

God Bless you all - Jeff

Chapter Sixty Eight

Smelling Gooood!

Posted May 27, 2009 8:02am

The last few days have been a little unusual, or so it seems. As I'm thinking back, some things seem opposite from day to day. And I'm getting some good, clear answers to prayer on some things that have been on my heart. The other day I took a shower (good start) and didn't even need the family intervention. I just did it. Anyway, my popularity level seemed to go up a little bit around the house. So, I'm pretty pleased that I finally took the plunge, literally.

Later that same day, Diane asked if I wanted to take a drive in the car and run a few errands. I think she invited me because I took a shower, had on a pair of jeans and I wasn't kicking around in my winter boots. I was looking good! I was hitting the road but first I needed to check the trunk. Ok, no shovel or tape measure so I guess the ride will be pretty safe.

I was making Diane some coffee this morning and somehow I had a whole counter full of water and coffee grounds. Hmm, something doesn't look right. Clean up on aisle seven! I need to hide the avocado knife too. I'll check the trunk. YEP, I'm still a mess! The coffee smells great but I now see a whole lot of water on the floor. Oh boy, this isn't looking good for the ol' Jeffers! It's a good thing my cousin Scott replaced my wall plugs with some GFI circuits last week because I'm looking to get a permanent perm if I'm not careful. By the way, the coffee smells great but it sure doesn't look right. I think I might get yelled at. Again! Uh oh. I need to put in my PMS eyes. And quickly!

Chapter Sixty Nine

Another Treatment

Posted May 29, 2009 7:21am

On Wednesday, Diane and I made another safe trip to and from treatment. It was a good day. My brother Vic was in town and he met us there. We had a nice visit with him and as always, it was nice to have a few good laughs with the queens of the chemo. Those fantastic nurses who take good care of us. All in all, the trip was pretty uneventful except for the elevator ride. I think someone knew I was in the building because the elevators were running in super-slow mode. Of course this means I was trapped inside the box o'funk longer than I was comfortable with. I wore my green mask and tried to look as sick as I could in hopes that no one would stand by me. Sporting my green mask and shuffling around like my shoelaces were tied together seemed to do the trick.

On the way home Diane stopped at the store so I waited in the car while she ran in and picked up a few things. Wow, it was sure warm in the car while the day's sun beamed down on me. I wonder if anyone reported to the store's management that there was a middle-aged man locked in a car in the parking lot? Yeah, he was crying and sweating profusely. I guess the sweatshirt, knit hat, and jacket may have been a little too much. I thought about getting out of the car for some fresh air but I was told to sit tight. So, I stayed put. I think Diane was worried that if I got out of the car I would wander off and get abducted. I would guess that any abductor would give me back as soon as they could. I mean, just looking at me they could tell they bit off more than they could chew. Hey, good news though, I did get a shower. While I was shaking and baking in the car, I didn't produce a foul odor. I sure wasn't looking good but I smelled good!

I gave the Lord a big thank you for the beautiful day, safe travel to treatment, and for the fact that Diane finally returned from the store and opened a window for me. Ahh, I can breathe again. So, I put away my PMS eyes and we were on our way. Have a blessed day and I'll talk to you soon. God bless you all! - Jeff.

Chapter Seventy

If

May 30, 2009

I'm not really sure what the future has in store for me. God only knows that. He knew on the day I was born what my purpose was and how many days I'd have to fulfill it. As of right now, I don't know what His plan is. I'm just trying to be faithful. When people heard I had brain cancer, I'm sure some immediately thought uh oh, God's mad at him. What did he do wrong? He's being punished. But since day one, I never had that thought. I know the Lord will do whatever it takes to bring a person into the right relationship with Him. I'm grateful He's done that because I have a good relationship with Him now and I've never felt I'm being punished. I'm just trying to deal with it and I'm learning a lot through it. It's not fun and it's not easy. But, it's become part of my life.

Everyday I feel grateful for the relationship I have with God. He has taught me a lot through this illness, which has been very helpful. Maybe I'm living that plan now. Maybe that plan will reveal itself after I pass away. I am in constant prayer with Him, always seeking His direction and asking for healing. It's a day-to-day battle. I am thankful and grateful for all that I have and all I am able to do. No one is going to live forever. Each of us will come to our final day.

I would like to share some of the challenges I've faced since my diagnosis. My first challenge was learning to accept the diagnosis. I never thought in a million years that I would get something like this. I thought it would be a motorcycle accident or old age, preferably old age. The diagnosis affected more than just me. Diane and the boys had to adjust their lifestyles in many ways as well. It's not a one-person illness as it affects many people. Some days are good and some are bad. Some days I wake up and feel good and, as I make my way to the kitchen, I start seeing signs or reminders of how I still have brain cancer. I see the Chemo schedule and all the bottles of medicine on the counter. It's a grim reminder that I have another day of dealing with this illness. Some days I'm a little bit angry and frustrated and, on the other days, I'm overwhelmed with gratitude. I am able to enjoy my days and find the brighter side of things. I learned so much just by watching my mom deal with the challenges of MS. She always looked for the positive side of everything and in every person.

It's a tough position to be in. I have heaven dangling in front of me and I know, when I get there, I'll wonder why I fought so hard to be here. I have two choices, hmmm… Heaven or the daily struggles and grind of this illness. It seems like a pretty simple choice. I feel excitement about heaven and then I feel despair with the thoughts of leaving Diane and the boys. There aren't too many treatment options left for me in this stage of the illness. All of my MRI scans over the past year, with the exception of one, have shown continued tumor progression. My next MRI is scheduled for this coming Wednesday. Based on my symptoms, I have a feeling it won't be good news. Even with that being said, I refuse to give up. I continue to pray the doctors will find the right combination of therapy to slow down or stop this tumor growth altogether. I don't want to give you the illusion that I go through my days whistling to the tune of "Whistle While You Work". But, throughout the day, I look at my situation and then I look at how it could be worse. It's then I can see my situation isn't so bad. It works wonders for any and all situations. You should give it a try. Do this everyday, and at the end of the day, you can't help but be thankful.

Chapter Seventy One

Merry Christmas in May

Posted May 31, 2009 8:26am

We had a beautiful day yesterday. The weather was very nice but I was pretty fatigued. I must admit I wasn't enjoying the day too much. I felt like a wind-up toy that wasn't getting wound up. I did make some of my world-famous egg salad and it came out pretty good. So, I did get something done. I even cleaned up my dishes. I asked Brett and Andrew if they wanted to have a picnic but Brett had to work. He's always so busy. But, I guess I was the same at his age, always working and running the roads. He'll learn to slow down a little and smell the roses. But, that will come in time and with age. We did do a quick kitchen picnic so the whole day wasn't lost. I guess it doesn't matter where you picnic.

It's just important to spend time with others and enjoy what you have, when you have it.

I wanted to take a walk to the mailbox yesterday but the distance looked too far away. The one hundred foot walk was out of my reach and I didn't think I could make the walk. I was getting exhausted just thinking about expending the energy to make the journey. I'll have to put it on my to-do list. It is kind of frustrating and discouraging. I would have never imagined that walking to the mailbox would be a challenge but I'm not giving up. I'll plan on walking out there today.

I'm thinking I could take next year's Christmas cards and mail 'em. I should probably get the belated ones. By the time I get the flag up they'll already be late. Merry Christmas 2010!! I guess a late card is better than no card. So, let me be the first to wish you a very Merry Christmas. Hmm, what if it starts to snow on me while I'm shuffling out to the mailbox? That would be weird but possible. Hey, I should wear my snow boots, you know, just in case. Also, I better put on some kind of diaper too so I don't get half way out there and have to turn back to answer nature's call. Wow, this trip to the mailbox may take some planning and rock solid coordination. I thought the trip to Vegas was tough but this one may be the toughest. It's a good thing I made some egg salad. I might need to pack a lunch. I guess, as a last ditch effort, I could catch a ride from the next person backing out of the garage. Hopefully they won't run me over first. I guess I should start wearing a hunter's orange vest from now on whenever I leave the house. You know the saying…safety first.

Well, I'm hopeful the fatigue will be kind to me today. And remember, the check is in the mail and I'm probably somewhere between the house and the mailbox. Have a blessed day and I'll try and mail you all a thank you card for your prayers, thoughts, and kind letters. We appreciate you all. One of my upcoming entries will be based on John 3:16 so keep your eyes open. Maybe I'll mail it. Thanks and God bless you all — Jeff, Andrew, Brett, and Diane.

Chapter Seventy Two

Clinical Trials

Posted May 31, 2009 6:43pm

Diane and I were just sitting around talking and I reminded her to make sure Andrew and Brett remember that, throughout my struggle with cancer, I NEVER gave up. I want them to know that I engaged these clinical trials in the hopes of being able to help others. Knowing that the trials were sometimes long shots, I was always hopeful that the doctors and the Tumor Board could learn something that would help other patients. At times, I felt like a Guinea Pig. Can a Guinea pig get the swine flu? Oh boy, where is my green mask? Hmm. Maybe I need the white one?

Well, here is how the clinical trial conversations went with the doctors, more or less. Ok Jeff, we see that the tumor is still growing so here's our plan. We have an open slot for a new trial called WF-7-10 and it might work. The slot came open because the last guy on it kicked the bucket. So, the slot is all yours. The WF-7-10 looks like this. The W - you'll drink some Weed -Be-Gagged for seven days and then experience some super-bad side affects for the next seven days. And, it's anyone's guess what will happen to you by day 10. Ok, sign here and we wish you the best. Well, we do know some of the side effects. Your gums will recede, your butt will itch like it's on fire, you'll grow hair on the palms of your hands, your hair will fall out, you'll have nose bleeds, sore throat, and dry skin. But we can give you some pills and ointment to counteract these minor inconveniences. In fact, you might be able to use what's in your murse. Ok, you just need to sign here. Please press hard and the third copy is yours. Good luck.

Well, that's kind of a crude version of the discussion but sometimes it sounded like that. I was always willing to do the trial in the hope that someone could benefit from my efforts. I wasn't looking to be a hero because, in the back of my mind, I was hoping it would work for me. But, I just felt that if my efforts could help someone else, then it was a risk worth taking. I still think that I made the right decisions in doing the clinical trials, as I'm sure that someone, somewhere has benefited from it. So, Brett and Andrew, remember that Dad kept up the good fight and I'll keep doing so. Keep me in your prayers and I'll keep fighting. God bless you both. – I love you. Dad.

Chapter Seventy Three

Is The Glass Half Full?

Posted Jun 2, 2009 7:09am

I can tell that today may be a little different than yesterday. I woke up this morning and felt more rested than I have in a long time. And it feels like a great way to start the day. I know that Diane talked with Dr. Roy and they talked about changing some of my medicine dosage. So, maybe that's in progress. I double-checked what she gave me yesterday and none of the pills looked like paint chips. Maybe she started me on the new dosage? I guess I'll have to wait and see. My friend DM (you know, the guy with the sand/dog poop on his shoe) was over yesterday. He said that the pills she gave didn't resemble paint chips so I guess I'll have to take his word on it.

Yesterday, I just couldn't seem to find any energy. But today, hopefully that will be different. Yesterday morning was a train wreck. It started early and made for a long day. First, I decided to mix up a breakfast drink. Sounds easy enough, right? What could go wrong with pouring a small packet of powder into a glass and adding milk? Well, let me tell you. The glass tumbler had a hole in the bottom so, as I added the milk, it drains onto the counter, into the drawer, and then onto the floor. I had a full-blown spilled milk crisis. So, I put in my crying-over-spilled-milk eyes and my day began. I had a huge mess in the kitchen again. I guess I might have to start finding a new hangout. If I create any more work for Diane, she might send me packing. Maybe she looks at it like some type of job security for her? I doubt it, but just maybe she does.

As I was pouring the milk into the glass and feeling it splash onto my shins I was thinking, surely I'm not missing the glass. What's going on here? Hmm. I'm a mess and Diane's kitchen is a mess too. I thought maybe if I turned the light off and hid behind the table I could blame someone else. But, since the milk was so deep, I couldn't swim that fast. I just cried and apologized profusely when she woke up. I don't think it helped when I asked her if she wanted a glass of instant breakfast that morning. But, she told me the mess wasn't as bad as I thought. I think she was just being kind because the milk went in the drawers too. So yesterday, the glass looked half empty. Actually, it started out half full, at least for a short time, until it drained out. If your glass is half full, pour some of the contents into someone else's glass and bless them. May the good Lord bless you and may your glass be full! I'll be in touch. – Love ya, Jeff.

Chapter Seventy Four

MRI Day

Posted Jun 4, 2009 9:14am

Yesterday was a family day at he the Hank. We all made the trek to the hospital for my scheduled MRI to see how the current treatment is working and, if it's holding this tumor at bay. The day was long as we ran back and forth to see Dr. Roy and Dr. D, squeezed in the MRI, had some lunch, did some blood work, and got some prescriptions filled. The to-do list seems never ending on these MRI days but we eventually headed home. I was exhausted by the end of the day. I felt like I had been working the valet parking line for a full shift. Yes, I did get to see my red-coated welcoming committee on this trip. But, Stacey drove so I didn't have to worry too much about the twelve cents she had in her console. The red jackets were a reminder that I had run the gauntlet between the safe outside air and the sess-pool of mixed funk that was waiting for me inside the hospital's walls.

Once I got there I felt a lot better because they gave me some paper pants to help protect me from any contamination that someone could have left in the tube. "Oh Jeff, after you put on these paper pants put on this paper jacket and this gown that doesn't close in the back and you'll be safe and isolated from any unsafe bacteria in the tube." Once you're dressed, or gowned up as they say, we'll get the MRI started. Yep, just lie in this tube for an hour and we'll be done. "We hope you're not claustrophobic because, if you are, it's going to be a long hour. Good, let's get started. Oh, if you have any metal in your body, the MRI will rip it from your skin and leave you in a world of hurt. So, good luck. Here we go." I'm now wondering if I should have been more generous to the valet guys? Will these coins I just had to have now cause me great bodily harm as it shreds my body and the nice paper pants I'm wearing? Well it didn't, so I was thankful for that. I guess I'll have to leave my red-jacketed friends a nice tip someday.

After they let me out of the tunnel of love, a.k.a. the MRI tube, we head upstairs to see Dr. Roy. He will review the results with us. Well, I'll fill you in on what we learned from the MRI scan. And the envelope says…some progression and some response; more front growth but the back growth has improved. There is also a new area in the Corpus Callosum, which is crossing over to the other side of the brain. The "Tumor Board" has decided to take me off the chemo but remain on the Avastin and start me on an anti-growth receptor (not a chemo drug) so I am hoping this fatigue will subside. I will have another MRI in 8 weeks. I also started on a new medication this morning that will help with my energy level. He said I am clinically doing well with only minor changes since the last MRI. He also said he was amazed, after looking at the MRI on the screen, that I was sitting there talking with him. He said, "Jeff you shouldn't be sitting here!" I'm not sure if he meant sitting here, meaning alive, or if he meant bed-ridden. But either way it only confirms to me what I have believed all along, God is in control. What better hands to be in! Amen

Chapter Seventy Five

My New Job

Posted Jun 12, 2009 6:39am

Have I been out job hunting? Well, not exactly. But, after a long discussion with my Lord during my last MRI, I decided to do something new. It's not a glamorous position, but it's the direction He told me to go. So, here I go. I'll be a letter and card writer to those needing encouragement. I know that I cannot get out to the hospitals to visit people in person but I can still make contact with them through greeting cards and letters. Plus, I wouldn't have to run through the gauntlet of rogue bacteria that is floating through the air and living on every surface at the hospital. Whew. Amen to that!

My mom always felt that this was something she could do so

maybe I'm picking up where she left off? I'll be a greeting card chaplain! It seems like it might work!

I did get some inspiration from my cousins, Uncle Jerry & Aunt Jackie, and a host of others who have sent me a quick note to let me know they're thinking of me. It's always uplifting! Hopefully I'll be able to help others as they are having a bad day and may need some encouragement. Thanks to my Uncle Bill & Cathy for tracking down some daily devotional books as I will try and incorporate them into my new job. You guys are great! I'll keep you posted as I get the process set up. Please keep your prayer requests coming so I can keep my list current with your friends and family members who are in need of prayer. I'll be in touch. Love ya, Jeff.

Chapter Seventy Six

The Trip

Posted Jun 13, 2009 5:20am

A few nights ago I thought it might be the evening that the Lord was going to take me home. But, as you can see, He didn't. I was beginning to doze off and was peacefully resting, very much at ease and excited. As I lay there it felt like my bags were packed, as if I was leaving for an out of town trip and I wasn't missing anything. I remember feeling excited, rested, and ready for the trip. I wasn't sure if I would have time to blog this but I wanted to be sure I passed it on. I told Diane and my buddy Tom to be sure they pass it on. But, it looks like I just did. I know that this old sinner will get to heaven because God so loved the world that He gave us His son who died on the cross for us. And, whoever believes in Him will not perish but have everlasting life!

May God bless you all and I hope to see you in heaven! I love you all – Jeff.

P.S. My new job isn't going so well. I think I'll need some help from my beautiful assistant, Diane. I'm trying to send condolence cards to folks who are still alive. So, either I'm really proactive or still needing some help. She'll get me on track. I'm doing well with the prayer list so, once I get my card process set up, this office will run smoothly. They may change my title to Sr. goof ball. I trust that the Lord knows what he's doing with me. Maybe I'm more willing than able but I won't give up. Love Jeff.

Chapter Seventy Seven

Prayers

Posted Jun 15, 2009 6:40am

Well, it was a busy day at my new job yesterday as there are many in need of prayer. I stayed faithful. And, since I was able to put my feet on the floor again this morning, I believe there is still more for me to do today. Yesterday was a frustrating day and, I must admit, I did find myself with an angry disposition at times. Sometimes my limitations really frustrate me. But, I have to focus on what I'm still able to do. Sometimes it feels like I'm being pulled in two directions. I try and focus on the good direction, which isn't always easy, and it helps. I know that things could always be worse so I'll keep pushing on. It isn't over yet. I know I probably sound like a broken record but, if something works, stick with it.

I did get outside for a short walk yesterday so that was a good sign. I didn't even have my snow boots on. I had my big boy shoes on. Laced up and everything. The sunshine felt nice. I had shoes on but I'm not sure if I had pants on. I'll have to ask Diane if I did. No one was yelling at me as they drove by so I think I was fully dressed. Hmm, I might have had my socks on my hands, my undies on my head, and my shirt on like a dress but at least I was dressed. God bless and I'll be in touch. – Love ya, Jeff

Chapter Seventy Eight

Coming Clean

Posted Jun 16, 2009 7:20am

Coming clean. Well, not in a soap and water clean but kind of a rinse in the sink clean. I need to share this. The other day I spent hours in conversation and prayer with my Lord and savior, Jesus Christ, in preparation to leave this earth and go to heaven. I was really prepared and ready. I was, and still am, at peace. I thought for sure He would have taken me by now but I woke up this morning and I'm still here. Hmm, I truly thought He would have taken me but here I sit. I am really surprised I'm here typing but here I sit. I guess it goes to show that He knows the plans He has for me. He just hired me to send cards to others and to be praying for them too. So, I'll stay committed to His call and do the best I can, even though everything I do is getting more difficult. He'll show me the way and provide me the help I need. He knows that there may still be a couple treatment options that are being looked at so maybe those will be his healing plan. I know that only He knows. I'll continue to wait on His healing touch and stay faithful to Him as I'm blessed with another day with my family, Diane, Brett, Andrew, my siblings, friends, family, and the list goes on and on. So Lord, give me the strength to make it through another day and thank you, Lord, for this day.

Please keep me in your prayers for healing and strength to get through each day. Also, let's pray for healing of my body. Thank you Lord and thank you all. May God bless you as He is totally blessing me. Please read John 3:16. I LOVE you all. Amen! I know heaven will be awesome but I'll have to go when my Lord is ready for me. It seems today I'll have to wait. God bless you all. Jeff. One more day with Diane! Cool! One more day with Andrew and Brett, too!

Chapter Seventy Nine

Up Again

Posted Jun 18, 2009 2:36pm

Well, the fatigue is really taking its toll. I was blessed and surprised with another day. I was blessed with some good conversation with Brett and Andrew. My brother Vic came and baby-sat me yesterday so it was a great day. I'm thankful for another day but I'm wearing out. Diane said she'd cover me in my new job since my letter writing skills are struggling. Let's see how this day turns out. May the Lord bless you all. Ok, I'll rest for a bit and thanks for all the blog feedback. I may not respond but I get your messages and I thank you all. Jesus loves you and so do I. I hope to see you all soon. – Jeff. Remember John 3:16. Thanks!

Chapter Eighty

Care Givers

This is one topic that I have wanted to discuss, but it's probably going to be one of the most difficult topics. Because, as you'll probably soon see, I will expose myself as a selfish and self-centered guy. I think it would be easier to throw myself under Miss Stacey's bus but, since she won't slow down, I'll just drag here from the bumper for a little while. I'm suspecting the outcome of this entry won't be pretty, but I think that others may be able to learn from, or at least understand, what this caregiver stuff is really all about.

My mother had Multiple Sclerosis and was well cared for by my little sister, Stacey. With Vic living in California and Ann-Marie living in Colorado, they would jump in and help by having Mom move in with them during alternating summers. Since I lived near Stacey, I would act as the back up and help out on some weekends or after hour times. Stacey would have probably been able to select a better back up, but she did the best she could with what she had, me! Stacey and Mike opened up their home to my Mom and made some special structural accommodations for her. They also made huge sacrifices in their daily lives to insure that she was well taken care of. Mike, Stacey, and their kids are true Saints and there are not enough words to tell you how much love, sacrifice, and time they invested in my mother. I am truly humbled by them. Victor and Ann-Marie have also taught me a lot about sacrifice and doing for others, so this entry is not getting any easier to write.

Diane is a wonderful caregiver. She keeps me on schedule for my appointments and my many medicines. The stool softener bottle is never empty and the toilet paper is always hanging. I think I saw that movie? Aside from my daily needs, there is an unbelievable amount of paperwork that she has to manage, such as work and insurance related documents and she somehow manages to keep it all together. If it was my responsibility and the shoe was on the other foot, we'd be living on the street and I'd be holding my "Will work for chemo" sign, just to get by. She has so much on her shoulders and she manages it all, everyday, with a great attitude and a smile in her heart. Should I be so lucky? I truly know why the Lord put me with her when we were a teenage Bride and Groom. She was nineteen and I twenty, and Andrew on the way. The Lord knew what He was doing then and we know that He still does. I doubted Him then but I don't doubt Him today.

Since I can still do most things for myself, I try and pitch in around the house as much as I can. The other day, Diane asked me to pick up my dirty underwear from the bedroom floor. I told her that I'm using them as navigational markers to help me walk around the room without bumping into dressers. She said, unless you're going to start navigating by smell, you need to get them up and into the hamper. So I did. See how helpful I am?

Getting back to Mom. Most things she couldn't do for herself. She was in a wheel chair and did not have the strength or motion to do everyday tasks, such as bathing, eating, getting dressed, and the huge list of things that I take for granted everyday. She never complained, although she had a lot she could have complained about. You know, the "why me" scenario?

How did I manage my role as caregiver? One word would sum it up. Poorly! On the days I was scheduled to take care of my Mom, I would be so filled with stress. I'm sure that my Mom could see this in my face. But I can only hope that she understood. When Stacey would drop my Mom off or I would pick her up, I felt that "my time" was over. I needed to cut the grass, paint the garage, and other things like that. If Mom was over, this was a big disruption in my schedule. I felt that I had too much to do and she would just be an added obligation. After this internal tug o-war, I would begin to have a huge infusion of guilt in my heart. I love her, so why am I feeling this way? I must be a bad person. The internal battle was like two dogs fighting. The dog that I fed the most usually won. It was exactly like being on an emotional roller coaster. I am not very proud of the times that I gave my mom the short end of stick or an unkind word that seemed to always bubble up over the weekend. I'm trying to get that important first cup of coffee on a Saturday morning, and then I hear my name being called from the spare bedroom. Jeeeeeeeeeeeeeeeefffffffff. Oh man. This means I have to get mom up, dressed, on the toilet, washed up, and fed. Wow, doesn't she know I need a coffee? Can't I just leave on the same shirt she just slept in? It smells ok. Maybe I can just recycle this brief she has on? Breakfast? Didn't she eat yesterday? Hmm, I have so much to do. I am thankful that I never sacrificed or short-changed the care of mom, such as eating and hygiene, but I'm sure the thought crossed my mind. Hmm, clean brief or a good cup of coffee?

Looking back, I am still upset by my attitude during my care-giving shifts. My brother and Sisters seemed to handle their shifts without incident while I, on the other hand, made my home an unsettled shell of a building. It seems that the act of care giving was not the problem, but rather the giving up of my time to do something for someone else. I know, sounds like the definition of selfish. I am really disappointed in my actions, but I have gained a lot of respect and compassion for those who find themselves in the role of caregiver. As in most situations it's a role that someone is thrust in to, as in Diane's case. I know she didn't sign up to be mine, but she is meeting the heavy challenge with so much grace. My daily prayer for her is for health and strength to continue with the new burdens that are piled on almost daily.

I love you Diane. I love Vic, Stacey, Ann-Marie, & Mike. Thanks for being so good to Mom. I know we all miss her daily. Diane would help with my Mom, but she felt that it was important that I, a male child, took an active role in mom's care giving. She told me that she gained a lot of respect for me. I don't know if it was because I was a boy and handled some of the not so delicate details of caring for someone or if she knew that some day I would possibly need the whole perspective of care giving or being cared for? I know that I'm definitely a better person for all the lessons I've learned while traveling the Care Giving highway. It was the people that have taught me the most, such as my nieces, nephews, brother's, sisters, wife, and my mom. I hope my sons caught a little of the lesson along the way, too. The good lesson, not the one where Dad freaked out because Grandma was asking for some more butter on her toast. As my Mom would remind me, I was a work in progress. If I keep progressing at this rate, I'll be backing up. Oh no, the last time I backed up Bob the Nurse was right behind me doing a cavity search in hopes of finding the missing trail mix from the nurses break room.

I'm thinking that care giving is a lot like trail mix. You never know what pieces you'll pick up, how you'll deal with it, or will it bind you up so bad that you'll think one of Nurse Bob's digital exams sounds like a pretty good time on a weekend? I think that anytime I can check out the Super bowl chair is not too bad. I wonder if Bob calls me puppet-boy?

Chapter Eighty One

Care giving

Posted Jun 19, 2009 4:34pm

Diane. ! Please post this for me. Never mind, I just did it on my own! I wanted to thank you for being s great csregiver, even if you mke me put on clean underwear after my shower. You are truly my best friend. Please post this for me. I thank you. You do so much for me and never complain. May Godcontinue to bless you! You are my best friend and always have been!!

Chapter Eighty Two

Jeff Update

Posted Jun 23, 2009 1:22pm

Hi, this is Jeff's brother, Vic. We wanted to let you know that Jeff is in Henry Ford Hospital. He has an infection in his neck/chin area. He's been having trouble with a tooth and we're not sure if that caused this infection or not. He is scheduled for surgery tomorrow to drain the infection. We'll keep you all posted on how everything goes. Sam said he put his foot in his mouth one too many times. Ha Ha Ha.

Chapter Eighty Three

Jeff

Posted Jun 24, 2009 6:55pm

Hi Everyone, the CT scan this morning showed tumor progression and bleeding in Jeff's brain. The Doctors said, due to the growth of the tumor and the swelling in the brain, the pressure could sometimes cause the brain to bleed. Needless to say the infection and abscess are the least of his problems now. So, they will not be doing any surgery. We met with Hospice today and Jeff has entered the Hospice program. Our main goal now is to manage his pain and make sure he is comfortable. The Doctors will evaluate Jeff tomorrow and make decisions at that time regarding the possibility of transferring Jeff to in-home Hospice care.

Although no one knows for sure, the Hospice nurse told us that without food and fluids we are looking at 1 to 21 days. Based on the bleed, the tumor progression, and the infection it will probably be sooner than later. Jeff is unresponsive but seems to be resting peacefully and appears to be comfortable and pain free.

As we sit here we can only think of all the funny blogs Jeff would write about this hospital stay. From the neon yellow socks that guarantee trouble if the nurses catch him walking in the hallway unassisted to the "condom catheter" that he is wearing. Or, the way Jeff would comment on the Detroit Freedom Festival Fireworks tonight … "I hope I'll be going out with a bang". We can just hear him going on and on!

Many thanks for the thoughts and prayers being sent this way. We will keep in touch.

Love, The family

Chapter Eighty Four

Jeff Ide - Dance and Shout

Posted Jun 25, 2009 4:59pm

Hi everyone, we are sitting in the hospital room with Jeff and were remembering a video that Diane shot of Jeff a few months ago. So, we thought we'd share it with you all. This song came on the radio; Jeff liked it, and started dancing. Diane grabbed the video camera and the rest is cinematic history. This is how Jeff dealt with brain cancer. Enjoy! If the link doesn't appear, just copy and paste the address below to your address bar.

http://www.youtube.com/watch?v=9enYNxsJM6o

Chapter Eighty Five

Update on Jeff

Posted Jun 27, 2009 7:18am

Hi everyone - we wanted to give you a quick update on Jeff. He came home from the hospital yesterday. Hospice set him up with a hospital bed and everything he needs so he can be at home for his final days. The Hospice folks are managing his pain and he seems to be sleeping well. We will keep you all posted.

Chapter Eighty Six

6/30/09

Posted Jun 30, 2009 1:32pm

Jeff is now entertaining all those in Heaven as he passed away around 1pm today. We will post funeral arrangements when they are complete. Thank you for all the prayers.

Chapter Eighty Seven

Jeff's Obituary

Posted Jun 30, 2009 6:16pm

Jeffrey Norman Ide, 44, of Riley Township, Michigan died Tuesday, June 30, 2009 at home surrounded by his family after a courageous battle with a cancerous brain tumor.

Jeff was born August 12, 1964 in Detroit, MI to the late Norman and Barbara (Steele) Ide of Capac, MI. He was married for 25 years to his high school sweetheart, Diane (Harvey). They were married on November 9, 1984 in Port Huron, MI. Jeff and Diane renewed their vows before Elvis on February 7, 2009 in Las Vegas, NV while on vacation with Jeff's brothers and sisters.

Jeff was a graduate of Sienna Heights University and was employed by Infineon Technologies in Livonia, MI as a

Quality Engineer. Jeff was a member of Zion Methodist Church in Capac and a member of Hogs in Ministry (HIM). This was a service organization where he raised money for many charities and continuously spread the word of God.

Jeff is survived by his wife, Diane and two sons, Andrew 24 and Brett 19 both of Riley, MI; in-laws Donald (Butch) and Linda Harvey of Bruceton, TN; a brother, Victor of San Francisco, CA and two sisters Ann-Marie Hennessy of Shelby Twp, MI and Stacey (Mike) Lauwers of Capac, MI; brother-in-law Donnie Harvey of Bruceton, TN and sisters-in-law Donna (Jim) Schmidlin of Yale, MI and Darla Harvey of Bruceton, TN; many aunts and uncles, nieces, nephews, cousins and friends.

He was preceded in death by parents Norman and Barbara Ide, brother-in-law Dion Harvey, grandparents Frank and Simone Ide of Detroit, MI and Walter R. and Margaret Steele of Capac, MI.

His family has chosen to honor the memory of Jeff and invite you to visit and share at the Richmond, MI Kaatz Funeral Home on Thursday, July 2, 2009 from 2pm-9pm and Friday, July 3, 2009 from 10am-11am with Funeral Services at 11am. Pastors Lisa Clark and Hal Phillips will officiate. Memorials are suggested to "Wishes of the family".

Chapter Eighty Eight

Final Words

The one common theme throughout Jeff's blogs was God. His incredibly strong faith and trust in God was his focus during his battle with brain cancer. As you can see, Jeff learned to appreciate more and give thanks more for the many blessings given to him by God. His focus turned more to the people and beauty around him and less on the material world. A lesson we all should try to learn without having to be faced with a devastating illness. How much better the world would be.

Jeff would sit and appreciate the way the trees looked against the sky and he even said that the birds sounded differently to him…perhaps he had finally taken the time to really listen to their song. As the days rush by, so many of us fail to appreciate the beauty and give thanks. Ironically, the day Jeff made the journey to heaven, we all were given the chance to feel God's presence through the beauty of His works.

Tuesday, June 30th was a gloomy day. Rains had been coming and going for the previous couple days and so the grey skies had still been present that day. Jeff's body was getting tired and we knew it wouldn't be long. Just after 1:00 pm, Jeff took his last breath with his family at his side. As Jeff's body lay there, we noticed a slight smile on his face. He looked peaceful and happy. It was a joy to witness his expression.

But that wasn't the best part. As Jeff was carefully lifted into the funeral home's van and the hatch door slowly closed, the sun came from behind the clouds and filled the sky with sunshine. A sign! OUR sign from God and Jeff that God had received Jeff into the kingdom of heaven and just wanted us to know. Jeff's faith and appreciation allowed us to recognize the beauty of the moment.... and it was only for a moment. Just as quickly as it appeared, the sun again retreated behind the clouds and remained there for the rest of the day.

From the day of his diagnosis, Jeff was always open to God's plan. Whether he was to receive healing on earth or the ultimate healing in heaven, Jeff was ready. On June 30, 2009 Jeff received the ultimate healing.

Jeff, Thank you for being such a faithful and devoted witness for God. May you rest in peace. We live with the assurance that one-day we will be together again. Eternal rest grant unto him O Lord, and let perpetual light shine upon him.

For God so loved the world, that He gave His only son, so that everyone who believes in Him might not perish but might have eternal life. John 3:16